Rockwell Lectures
Rice University

**The American Search
for Soul**

The American Search for Soul

ROBERT S. MICHAELSEN

Louisiana State University Press
Baton Rouge

ISBN 0–8071–0097–8
Library of Congress Catalog Card Number 74–82005
Copyright © 1975 by Louisiana State University Press
Manufactured in the United States of America
Designed by Albert Crochet

Grateful acknowledgment is made for permission to
use material in Chapter 2 that originally appeared as
"Americanization: Sacred or Profane Phenomenon?"
Reconstructionist, XXXVII (May 7, 1971), 7–16.

To my father and my sons

Contents

Preface

Soul is a rich word. It has a variety of meanings and nuances. In these pages it will be used variously: as the "animating principle," "moving spirit," or "actuating cause" of a person, a movement, or a nation (chapter one); as the "essential element" in the identity of a man, a movement, or a nation (chapter two); and as the "spiritual part of man considered in its moral aspect or in relation to God" (chapter three). The last definition suggests a possible division that does not do justice, however, to the fullness of meaning the word has had in the Western world, even when used in a specifically religious context. For *soul* has been understood most significantly in this context to mean fundamentally not a part of a person but "a person's total self in its living unity and wholeness."[1]

This work is informed by an assumption that, to do justice to the subject, a discussion of American self-understanding must come to an analysis of the role of religious experience and assumptions in that self-understanding. G.

1. Quotations from the *Random House Dictionary of the English Language*, *Webster's Third New International Dictionary*, and the *Oxford Dictionary of the English Language*.

K. Chesterton once asserted that America is "a nation with the soul of a church."[2] That means not only that Americans have generally been religiously active and concerned people, but also that they have understood the founding, purpose, and destiny of their nation within a cosmic religious context. This has made for an intricate fabric consisting of a warp of personal and denominational religious experiences and convictions and a weft of national religious self-understanding. The fabric is made even more complex by virtue of the fact that it has been woven on a loom that, in its formal structure, precludes state "establishment of religion" or prohibition of the "free exercise thereof."[3] This book is an analysis of these complex interrelations within the context of what I take to be our present crisis in national self-understanding. Obviously the analysis is both modest and perspectival in nature, and the book may best be seen as a participant-observer's report.

This volume is a much revised and augmented version of lectures delivered under the title "The Crisis in American Faith and Learning" at Rice University in February, 1973. I express here my gratitude to Professor Niels Nielsen and his colleagues in the Department of Religion and to Mr. Henry Rockwell, sponsor of the oldest continuing lectureship at Rice, for their gracious and kind hospitality in making my stay in Houston a delightful occasion.

I am also grateful to Professors Louis K. Dupré and Robert T. Handy and to my wife Florence for sharing with me their suggestions concerning the manuscript. I, of course, accept full responsibility for the final result.

Robert Michaelsen
University of California
Santa Barbara
October, 1974

2. G. K. Chesterton, *What I Saw in America* (New York: Dodd, Mead and Company, 1922), 11.
3. *United States Constitution*, First Amendment.

1

New World Soul: As Conceived and in Crisis

Novus ordo seclorum—a new society for this world
Annuit coeptis—our undertaking is favored
　　　　　—Affirmations on the Great Seal of the United States

"We have it in our power to begin the world over again."
　　　　　　　　　　　　　　　　—Thomas Paine

"So let us begin anew."—John F. Kennedy

It was possible to begin anew. In this New World men and women could begin over again; a new type of human being could emerge; and these new creatures could build a new society, which would be the kind that aspiring people had longed for since the original creation. America thus excited the imagination of the Western world, and the vision of soul potential in the New World was a product of that imagination. Twice-born Americans—the immigrants—were led by that vision. They, in turn, embellished it both for the Old World and the New. And birthright Americans, as if with pristine eyes, saw this vision as their own.

"What is this American . . . this new man?" asked Michel de Crèvecoeur in the eighteenth century. He was new, he was different, and he was what the West had long sought. Here in this New World the "Western pilgrims" would "finish the great circle." Here men of all nations would be transformed into "a new race of men."[1] A century and a half later this same sentiment still loomed large in American self-perception. America was "God's crucible," de-

1. Michel de Crèvecoeur, *Letters from an American Farmer* (New York: E. P. Dutton and Company, 1951), 40—45.

1

clared Israel Zangwill in his popular play *The Melting-Pot.*
From that crucible would emerge a new kind of man, "the
real American," who would be "the fusion of all races,
perhaps the coming superman."[2]

The stage was set for a new creation. There was space—
both physical and social. That meant openness, freedom
from the confining restrictions of old ways. This New
World beckoned like light at the end of a long tunnel. It
suggested hope, promise, a better future; indeed, this New
World promised a transformed future, which would be as
different from the past as brilliant sunshine is different
from the darkness of a tunnel. In the minds of men, the
sense of unoccupied space (the natives could be swallowed
up, moved, or exterminated) was transformed from physical to spiritual reality, or perhaps the physical openness
made possible a dramatic spiritual transformation—an unprecedented changeabout. Mircea Eliade rightly points out
that "the discovery and colonization of the New World
took place under the sign of eschatology."[3] Here all things
would be made new; here all things seemed possible.

The Founding Fathers, fully confident that their new
beginning was especially favored (*annuit coeptis*), boldly
opted for a this-worldly eschatology. They declared their
intention to build the *novus ordo seclorum*, the new society for this world, and to secure here in this world the
"blessings of liberty" for themselves and their posterity.
Earlier Americans had expressed in religious terms, but not
without worldly effect, a somewhat similar intention—to
build a "biblical commonwealth" or to restore primitive
Christianity in this New World.[4] Jonathan Edwards

2. Israel Zangwill, *The Melting-Pot: A Drama in Four Acts* (New
York: Macmillan Company, 1911), 37–38.

3. Mircea Eliade, *The Quest: History and Meaning in Religion*
(Chicago: University of Chicago Press, 1969), 89.

4. The early American Puritans generally thought of themselves
as being involved in the establishment of both church and state in
accordance with the biblical pattern. William Penn embarked on his

merged the Christian motif with the New World environment in his eschatological vision of the ripening in America
of the first fruits of the kingdom of God.[5]

Whether the eschatology was clearly religious or mani-
festly secular, the expectation was great. It is not easy to
recover today the sense of excitement that this new venture released. The discovery and settlement of the New
World exhilarated the Western mind. Americans thrived on
this excitement, and the enthusiasm of countless emigrants
from the Old World was enkindled by it. America promised or resembled a spiritual experience. "The immigrant's
arrival in his new home is like a second birth to him," said
Abraham Cahan through the lead character in his novel
The Rise of David Levinsky.[6] Another immigrant novelist,
Ole Rölvaag, wrote in *Giants in the Earth* of the frenzy
that had seized the "Western pilgrims" in their relentless
pursuit of a promised but elusive Eden: "Here on the
trackless plains, the thousand year old hunger of the poor
after human happiness had been unloosed."[7]

Expectation and enthusiasm bred self-confidence. Alexis
de Tocqueville was a friendly and, at times, even enthusiastic viewer of the American scene. Yet even he grew impa-
tient with American self-assurance. Observed Tocqueville:

> If I say to an American that the country he lives in is a fine one,
> "Ay," he replies, "there is not its equal in the world." If I
> applaud the freedom that its inhabitants enjoy, he answers:

"holy experiment" in the New World with the full conviction that
the religion that he professed was "primitive Christianity revived."
See his treatise of that title in J. Fothergill (ed.), *The Select Works of
William Penn* (New York: Kraus Reprint Company, 1971), II,
471–512.

5. C. C. Goen (ed.), *The Works of Jonathan Edwards: The Great
Awakening* (New Haven: Yale University Press, 1972), 353.

6. Abraham Cahan, *The Rise of David Levinsky* (New York:
Harper and Brothers, 1960), 86–87.

7. Ole Rölvaag, *Giants in the Earth: A Saga of the Prairie,* trans.
Lincoln Colcord and Ole Rölvaag (New York: Harper and Row,
1964), 227.

"Freedom is a fine thing, but few nations are worthy to enjoy it."
If I remark on the purity of morals that distinguishes the United
States, "I can imagine," he says, "that a stranger, who has
witnessed the corruption that prevails in other nations, would be
astonished at the difference." At length I leave him to the
contemplation of himself; but he returns to the charge and does
not desist till he has got me to repeat all I had just been saying. It
is impossible to conceive a more troublesome or more garrulous
patriotism; it wearies even those who are disposed to respect it.[8]

This same self-confidence characterized the American re-
formers. Was there anything wrong in the nation? It could
be righted. "We are all a little wild here with numberless
projects of social reform," Ralph Waldo Emerson wrote to
Thomas Carlyle in 1840. "Not a reading man but has a
draft of a new community in his waistcoat pocket."[9]

Coming into the New World was not only like seeing
light at the end of a tunnel; it was like emerging from
Plato's cave. Here and now one could see the good, *and*
one could *do* it. Not only would society be changed;
human nature itself would be made over. The ocean passage, like the later western trek, brought transformation.
Scales dropped from the eyes; old prejudices disappeared;
tribalisms declined; crabbed self-centeredness gave way to
a refreshing openness. This new nation marked the launching of "a new era" in human history, proclaimed Horace
Mann early in the nineteenth century. Now one could
"expect a new series of developments in human nature and
conduct."[10]   Less than a century later Woodrow Wilson
expressed much the same confidence when he professed to
see true Americans as "purged of the more debased and
selfish elements of human ambition" and, hence, an inspi-

8. Alexis de Tocqueville, *Democracy in America* (New York:
Vintage Books, 1954), II, 236.
9. Quoted in Winthrop S. Hudson, *Religion in America* (New
York: Charles Scribner's Sons, 1965), 181.
10. Mrs. Mary Mann (ed.), *Life and Works of Horace Mann* (Boston: Lee and Shepard, 1891), II, 14, IV, 8.

ration to all aspiring men. "Americans must have a consciousness different from the consciousness of every other nation in the world," Wilson declared. Americans were different and, by implication or direct assertion, they were or could be better than what had gone before.[11]

This vision of a newborn soul in America was supported by an ideology that affirmed the uniqueness and universal significance of the American enterprise. To gather support for their endeavors, the Founding Fathers appealed to every universalizing and hence ultimately ratifying principle they knew: to nature and nature's God; to divine providence; to human reason; and to the "opinions of mankind."[12] They pictured themselves enacting a drama of universal significance—forming and reforming human nature and the society intended by nature itself and longed for by all thoughtful men. Since independence, American self-understanding has been dominated by this sense of the uniqueness and the universality of the American mission. It spawned the notion of manifest destiny. It dominated American self-consciousness in world affairs. It fell naturally from the lips of politicians, preachers, and poets alike. "We Americans are a peculiar chosen race," said Herman Melville. "We bear the ark of the liberties of the world."[13]

Presidential utterances abound with this same sense of chosenness, uniqueness and destiny. Abraham Lincoln, one of the soberer and more sensitive of the nineteenth-century political leaders, expressed this idea in a more restrained and humble fashion than was customary when he referred to Americans as God's "*almost* chosen people."

11. Ray Stannard Baker and William E. Dodd (eds.), *The Public Papers of Woodrow Wilson* (New York: Harper and Brothers, 1925–27), III, 132, 321.
12. Declaration of Independence.
13. Quoted in Dorothy Dohen, *Nationalism and American Catholicism* (New York: Sheed and Ward, 1967), 12.

Still, Lincoln's sense of destiny led him to paint the Civil
War on a cosmic canvas. Americans, he said, could not
escape history in that war; by their actions they would
"nobly save, or meanly lose, the last best, hope of
earth."[14] Woodrow Wilson, a less sober observer than
Lincoln, used a similar canvas on which to portray America's role in the grand design of human destiny. He colored
American participation in World War I in terms of unself-
ishness and identification with the real interests of men
everywhere. It was a war to make the world safe for
democracy.[15] A generation later John F. Kennedy, although seeing himself as part of a generation whose idealism was more realistic than that of his predecessors, still
had recourse to the same global vision. He sought to
recruit not only his fellow Americans but also his "fellow
citizens of the world" in "a struggle against the common
enemies" and for the common goals of all mankind.[16]

That the American venture should be seen as unique is
not particularly surprising. This is one of the character-
istics of nationalism. Even the universalistic claim, which is
not a common characteristic of nationalism, was not new
or unique to America. It was a sentiment that was much
articulated in its egalitarian form by the eighteenth-century French philosophers, whose thought influenced the
publicists of both the American and the French revolutions. What was more unusual was the emergence in this
new nation—which was without a unified national history,
a uniform religious history, or an established church—of a

14. Paul M. Angle and Earl Schneck Miers (eds.), *The Living
Lincoln* (New Brunswick, N.J.: Rutgers University Press, 1955), 378,
522. Emphasis added.
15. See, for example, Wilson's address to a joint session of the two
houses of Congress, April 2, 1917, on the occasion of the declaration
of war against Germany.
16. Davis Newton Lott (ed.), *The Presidents Speak: Inaugural
Addresses of the American Presidents from Washington to Nixon*
(3rd ed.; New York: Holt, Rinehart and Winston, 1969), 271.

theological and moral consensus that supported the American sense of uniqueness. This consensus in American beliefs, which made up the common core of what Professor Sidney E. Mead confidently calls "the religion of the Republic,"[17] consisted of certain assumptions or convictions about God, man, and immortality. Nearly everyone in the late eighteenth century, from stringent Calvinists to radical deists, affirmed or assumed (1) that the universe was created and is governed by an all-powerful God who is worthy of reverence and is the judge of human action; (2) that man is required by this God to do good in this life; and (3) that there is a future life in which men will be rewarded or punished on the basis of their actions in this world. Theological debate raged over the nature of God, but few denied his existence or his roles as creator, providential guide, and judge. Men disagreed sharply over human capacity for doing good, but none denied the importance of morality or virtue in human action, and few denied that virtue would be rewarded and vice punished in a life beyond death. There were many opinions about the manner of conversion or salvation, but most agreed that men could be radically changed for the better. And most saw America as an extraordinarily fruitful context for such a change.

These fundamentals of American belief were closely akin to the basic tenets of that form of rational religion, or deism, that had first emerged in England in the seven-

17. Sidney E. Mead, "The 'Nation with the Soul of a Church,' " *Church History*, XXXVI (1967), 262–83, esp. 275. See also Mead's *The Lively Experiment: The Shaping of Christianity in America* (New York: Harper and Row, 1963); "The Post-Protestant Concept and America's Two Religions," *Religion in Life*, XXXIII (1964), 191–204; and "The Fact of Pluralism and the Persistence of Sectarianism," in Elwyn A. Smith (ed.), *The Religion of the Republic* (Philadelphia: Fortress Press, 1971). See also other essays in the Smith volume, especially John Wilson's challenge to the notion of "civil religion," 1–21.

teenth century and had become increasingly more influential among European and American intellectuals in the
eighteenth century. Lord Herbert of Cherbury (1583–
1648) set forth in 1645 the religious "Common Notions"
that were to be articulated or assumed by all succeeding
deists: (1) There is one supreme God; (2) he ought to be
worshiped; (3) virtue and piety are the chief parts of divine
worship; (4) men ought to be sorry for their sins and
repent of them; and (5) divine goodness dispenses rewards
and punishments, primarily on moral grounds, both in this
life and the next.[18] These notions were essentially the
same as those expressed by Benjamin Franklin on more
than one occasion, although Franklin stressed even more
than Herbert had the centrality of "doing good" in response to the deity and in anticipation of future reward. [19]
These ideas were also shared by Thomas Jefferson, George
Washington, and Thomas Paine.[20]

Deism was not popular among eighteenth-century Protestant pietists and evangelicals, however. Indeed, it was
anathema, and openly articulate deists, such as Paine,
Jefferson, and Voltaire and his French associates, were
attacked as infidels. Partially because of this antipathy,
deism had little success as a religious movement in the new
nation. But the tendency to declare certain religious fundamentals common to all men and to find these fundamen-

18. See the article "Deism" in the *Encyclopedia of Philosophy*, II,
326–36.
19. On Franklin's religious views see L. Jesse Lemisch (ed.), *Benjamin Franklin: The Autobiography and Other Writings* (New York:
New American Library, 1961), 318–38, and Alfred Owen Aldrige,
Benjamin Franklin and Nature's God (Durham, N.C.: Duke University Press, 1967).
20. On the beliefs of the Founding Fathers see Norman Cousins
(ed.), *In God We Trust: The Religious Beliefs and Ideas of the
American Founding Fathers* (New York: Harper and Brothers,
1958). On deism in America see Gustav A. Koch, *Republican Religion: The American Revolution and the Cult of Reason* (New York:
Henry Holt and Company, 1933), and Herbert M. Morais, *Deism in
Eighteenth-Century America* (New York: Russell and Russell, 1960).

tals supportive of and essential to the new American venture was continuous. Furthermore, it is surprising how much of a hold the essentially deist notions gained among Americans, especially when they addressed themselves to issues of public policy and formation.

Efforts to identify a *specific* historical religious tradition with the American enterprise were generally resisted. When Christianity was put forward as being essential to the public weal, it was usually advanced in a generalized rather than a specific form. The word *Christian* was often used to mean moral or good or even reasonable. By the late nineteenth century some articulate Christian spokesmen were even glad to settle for a generalized religion as the essential element for human integrity in America. Josiah Strong, author of the widely read *Our Country*, argued that there were "three great fundamental doctrines which are common to all monotheistic religions" and which were essential to the moral and civic role of the common school. These doctrines were "*the existence of God, the immortality of man* and *man's accountability.*"[21] Benjamin Franklin would have approved.

By the mid-twentieth century this tendency to stress certain religious fundamentals relative to public policy and formation had been distilled into common "moral and spiritual values." Dwight D. Eisenhower, who was the most symbolically significant American of that period, buttressed these values with a generalized faith. In so doing he aligned himself squarely with the eighteenth-century Founding Fathers and with prevailing American self-understanding. Like the Founding Fathers, he wanted to trace that self-understanding to an ultimate spiritual source. He

---

21. Josiah Strong, *Our Country*, ed. Jurgen Herbst (Cambridge: Harvard University Press, 1963), 98. By the time Strong wrote these words in the late nineteenth century, most evangelicals saw American civilization and Christian civilization as two sides of the same coin. See Robert T. Handy, *A Christian America: Protestant Hopes and Historical Realities* (New York: Oxford University Press, 1971).

described America's role in World War II as a moral and spiritual crusade to turn back the forces of wrong and evil. And he easily reverted to similar language to describe America's role in the cold war that followed. He clearly affirmed that the goals of each crusade were right because they were grounded in the nature of things. But he also declared that success in achieving those goals depended finally on a deeply held spiritual faith. He saw the American stress on human spirituality to be unique among nations but at the same time universally and ultimately significant.[22]

Kenneth Boulding, American economist and philosopher, is reported to have said that "if he could 'explain' President Eisenhower satisfactorily, he would hold the key to the meaning of human history."[23] An obvious instance of hyperbole, this statement nevertheless rightly suggests that an understanding of Eisenhower could go a long way toward helping one to understand American self-perception at least to recent times. However imprecise his language might have been, Eisenhower did manage to project what was to many a remarkably convincing image of New World soul.

CRISIS

By the time Eisenhower had passed from the American scene, however, the ultimate ground seemed in dissolution,

22. On Eisenhower's religious views see Paul Hutchinson, "The President's Religious Faith," *Christian Century*, LXXI (March 24, 1954), 362–69. For critical treatments see William Lee Miller, *Piety Along the Potomac: Notes on Politics and Morals in the Fifties* (Boston: Houghton Mifflin, 1964), esp. 125–31, and Will Herberg, *Protestant, Catholic, Jew* (Garden City, N.Y.: Doubleday and Company, 1955); for a more sympathetic treatment, which sees Eisenhower in the context of the eighteenth-century Founding Fathers, see Mead, "The Post-Protestant Concept and America's Two Religions," and "The 'Nation with the Soul of a Church.'" On the Eisenhower phenomenon and its possible significance see Charles L. Sanford, *The Quest for Paradise: Europe and the American Moral Imagination* (Urbana: University of Illinois Press, 1961).
23. Quoted in Sanford, *The Quest for Paradise*, 1.

and the uniqueness and universality of the American claim were subjected to unprecedented doubt. Perhaps there was more than coincidence in the confluence of rumors of the "death of God" with Eisenhower's own demise. By that time Americans had also to cope with the violent deaths of three of their most eloquent, younger articulators of an inclusive American idealism—the two Kennedys and Martin Luther King, Jr. One felt that an era had ended and that the soul of America was in deep distress.

American beliefs had, of course, been tested before. Even news of the presumed death of God was not exactly new. Articulate Americans had previously called attention to the erosion of theological certainties under the attack of what one such observer had called in 1929 "the acids of modernity."[24] Still, that theistic belief had displayed a remarkable hardiness, even into the 1960s. What happened then was not only the result of an undermining of theistic faith; it was the culmination of a series of blows that challenged all of the essentials of American self-perception—not only the idea of God, but morality, immortality, and the fundamental notions of the uniqueness and universality of the American mission.

For a quick overview of the factors leading to this culmination, one needs to go no further back in American history than the late nineteenth century when, primarily under the impact of Darwinism, America experienced an intellectual revolution. "Darwinism," said B. J. Loewenberg, "attacked the whole American *Weltanschauung.*"[25] It appeared to undermine the notion of ultimate and universal design and hence to raise serious doubts about a transcendent and providential deity, the uniqueness of man, and a purposive immortality—in other words, the

24. Walter Lippmann, *A Preface to Morals* (New York: Macmillan Company, 1929), 8.

25. B. J. Loewenberg, "Darwinism Comes to America, 1859–1900," *Mississippi Valley Historical Review*, XXVIII (1941), 339–68, esp. 339.

fundamentals of American belief. The theologically conservative Charles Hodge went to the heart of the matter
when he argued that Darwin denied design and then drew
the logical conclusion that "Darwinism is atheism."[26]

But the zealous theological compromisers of the late
nineteenth century sought to rescue design and God by
identifying God with the evolutionary process itself. God
became immanent and evolution progressive.[27]   That
seemed to save another eighteenth-century confidence:
that the new was better than the old. But the eighteenth
century believed that the new was better than the old
because it more nearly approximated the primeval, the
original, the paradigmatic—in fact, nature itself. And by
nature the men of the Enlightenment meant pattern, regu-
larity, law—that which was designed by the divine architect
and built and regulated by the divine engineer. To identify
God with the evolutionary process was to open up a whole
new set of theological and moral speculations. Pattern
seemed in doubt, except that claimed for the evolutionary
process itself. But the pattern suggested by the evolutionary process did not correspond with the eighteenth-century understanding of nature. Among other things, the
notion of an original human rationality and morality was
hardly supported by evolution. Man was descended from
lower species, he was a predator, and he relentlessly pursued his own survival.

26. Charles Hodge, *What Is Darwinism?* (New York: Scribner,
Armstrong, and Company, 1874), 177.
27. For an analysis of what I call the "zealous theological compro-
misers," see Ira V. Brown, "Lyman Abbott: Christian Evolutionist,"
New England Quarterly, XXIII (1950), 218–31; Frank Hugh Foster,
*The Modern Movement in American Theology: Sketches in the
History of American Protestant Thought from the Civil War to the
World War* (New York: Fleming H. Revell Company, 1939), Chap. 3;
Richard Hofstadter, *Social Darwinism in American Thought* (Rev.
ed.; Boston: Beacon Press, 1955); and Stow Persons, "Evolution and
Theology in America," in Stow Persons (ed.), *Evolutionary Thought
in America* (New Haven: Yale University Press, 1950), 422–53.

The eighteenth-century confidence in human rationality and in the universality of moral law was dealt a further blow by the increasing awareness that peoples differed radically in what they regarded as right and wrong. Universal, rational moral principles seemed in danger, and that posed a threat to the assumed uniqueness and universality of the American enterprise. If one acknowledged cultural relativity, then the American enterprise must be seen as but one among many human endeavors and without legitimate claim to either uniqueness or universality.

This chain of challenges and doubts was slow in being linked, however. In fact, it was long resisted. Generalized faith could be maintained so long as it remained sufficiently generalized. It appeared to make little difference whether that faith was associated with a master architect and engineer or with the process of evolution. Above all, despite some disquietude over the apparent rawness of the human drive to survival and over cultural relativity, morality seemed as secure as the Rock of Gibraltar.[28]

A Belgian theologian, Count Eugène Goblet d'Alviella, who studied religious conditions in America in the 1880s when the impact of Darwinism was first being felt, was surprised to discover that American clergy generally placed more emphasis on morals than on theology.[29] Interest in

28. On moral confidence in the late nineteenth century see George Santayana, *Character and Opinion in the United States: With Reminiscences of William James and Josiah Royce and Academic Life in America* (Charles Scribner's Sons, 1920), Chap. 1, and Henry F. May, *Protestant Churches and Industrial America* (New York: Harper and Brothers, 1949), "The Summit of Complacency," Pt. 2. Donald H. Meyer's *The Instructed Conscience: The Shaping of the American National Ethic* (Philadelphia: University of Pennsylvania Press, 1972) is a useful work based on a study of college texts on moral philosophy written in the United States in the mid-nineteenth century.

29. Count Goblet wrote: "If one reads to-day in the American journals of Monday the report of the principal sermons preached the preceding day by the ministers of the different sects [and such reports were common features of Monday editions of newspapers in

theological doctrine was perfunctory, but inculcation and enhancement of morality were clearly regarded as fundamental. God might change, but morality remained fixed. Religion was understood by many to consist of morality tinged with sentiment.

There had developed in America, by the late nineteenth century, a moral confidence that seemed almost impervious to change. Industry, supported by such other republican virtues as honesty, frugality, and temperance, paid off, or so it seemed. The Ten Commandments and the Golden Rule appeared admirably to embody the standards of common decency. The true American had apparently been fully formed. This American, this "new man," was active, industrious, and honest—common in class or origin but most uncommon in ambition and virtue.

William Holmes McGuffey, through his famous *Eclectic Readers*, had mixed liberal elements of the wisdom of Poor Richard (industry plus frugality equals wealth and virtue) into the common fare of the common schools. He had anointed the mixture with heavenly unction and liberally seasoned it with patriotic zeal. The result was a moral system that consisted of the Ten Commandments and the Golden Rule, augmented by the work ethic and patriotic piety, sanctified by a benevolent deity, and reinforced by the promise, or threat, of a future life.

For well over a century this moral system was a primary element in American self-perception and a standard feature in the common schools. Few men could flaunt it and maintain any kind of status in the body politic. Perhaps the most serious threat to this system in the nineteenth century was the Mormon advocacy and practice of plural

the late nineteenth century], he will be surprised to see the small place which theology occupies compared with morals." Count Eugène Goblet d'Alviella, *The Contemporary Evolution of Religious Thought in England, America, and India*, trans. J. Moden (London: Williams and Norgate, 1885), 203.

marriage. (The Civil War was supported by both sides in the name of the moral system.) That practice was considered sufficiently flagrant to justify Supreme Court condemnation, despite the fact that it was done in the name of religion. In fact, this religious advocacy made the practice doubly offensive. It flew in the face of the morality the eighteenth-century Founding Fathers had thought to be universal and divinely sanctioned. In 1890 the Court settled the issue by denying that such an outrageous practice as plural marriage could be based on religion, properly understood, and by branding it as being contrary to the "common sense of mankind."[30] Hence the Court stood squarely and relentlessly on the fundamental assumption that the American moral system, with its sanction of monogamy, was identical with that universal moral system supported by both God and all men of "common sense."

After 1890 the Mormons fell in with nearly all other religious groups in supporting the American moral system. Roman Catholic moralists tended to be as stringent as Protestant moralists in support of that system. Even liberal groups embraced it; in fact, one might say that the Unitarians especially became experts in common decency. Octavius Brooks Frothingham recalled in 1891 that at Harvard Divinity School, even at mid-century, religion was understood to be more a matter of morality than spirituality. [31] It is not surprising that the graduates of this school also preached morality.

Frothingham also pointed out that at Harvard in his student days "an inward 'experience of religion' . . . was not demanded."[32] Count Goblet might have observed that

30. *Davis* v. *Beason*, 133 U.S. 333 (1890).
31. Octavius Brooks Frothingham, *Recollections and Impressions, 1822–90* (New York: G. P. Putnam's Sons, 1891), 25. A Unitarian clergyman, Frothingham was one of the founders of the Free Religious Association.
32. *Ibid.*

the same was true of many of the preachers he had heard.
He might also have noted that even when such an experience was demanded, as in the revival system, conversion
clearly entailed wholehearted commitment to the accepted
moral system. Conversion had become so thoroughly routinized and standardized, in fact, that few surprises were to
be expected. And the greatest soul winner of them all,
Dwight Lyman Moody, was a perfect embodiment of the
active virtues of the American moral system. He expected
his converts also to practice the same virtues.

This is not to belittle the prodigious accomplishments or
the impressive character of Dwight L. Moody. The point is
rather that in Moody one sees a clear example of the
inseparability of evangelical religion, conventional morality, and public piety.[33] Revivalism and moralism now
went hand-in-hand. That might not be an occasion for
surprise; after all, does not religion support morality?
Clearly it has been a common assumption in the Western
world that the connection between religion and morality is
axiomatic. While this is a question worthy of substantial
treatment, suffice it to suggest at this point and on the
authority of no less a figure than Alfred North Whitehead

33. On Moody, revivalism, and the status quo, see Bernard A.
Weisberger, *They Gathered at the River: The Story of the Great
Revivalists and Their Impact upon Religion in America* (Boston:
Little, Brown and Company, 1958), 175–78. Moody, writes Weisberger, "completed the reduction of evangelism to a matter of
technique and personality. . . . Moreover, Moody was outdated. In
technique, he was a creature of his age, but in faith he belonged to
the half century which preceded him. . . . His preaching froze a part
of American Christianity into nostalgia." William G. McLoughlin,
Jr., concludes in *Modern Revivalism: Charles Grandison Finney to
Billy Graham* (New York: Ronald Press Company, 1959), 167, that
"the most striking feature of Moody's outlook and of all modern
revivalism in the years between the Civil War and the First World
War, was its conservatism." The most thorough and scholarly biography of Moody is James F. Findlay, Jr., *Dwight L. Moody:
American Evangelist, 1837–1899* (Chicago: University of Chicago
Press, 1969).

that "morality, in the petty negative sense of the term, is the deadly enemy of religion." In fact, Whitehead points out, "the great religions of civilisation include among their original elements revolts against the inculcation of morals as a set of isolated prohibitions."[34] By the late nineteenth century, however, religion had become quite well domesticated and moralized in America. Major revolts seemed unlikely to occur.

The most able student of religion at that time, William James, thought it necessary to look beyond traditional religious forms and institutions for the most vital religious phenomena. The essence of religion, he thought, was to be found in mystical and psychical experience, not in institutions, theological formulas, or moral systems. In fact, James recognized the "radical discord" between true religion and moralism. Life is tenuous and threatening, James knew, and in the end "all our morality appears but as a plaster hiding a sore it can never cure."[35]

Yet James himself seems to have opted for moralism. Mystical experiences seem to have been of little or no importance in his own life. He was not without what a later psychologist has called "peak experiences," but even these seemed to reinforce his commitment to the American moral system.[36] George Santayana, an unfriendly

34. A. N. Whitehead, *The Aims of Education and Other Essays* (London: Ernest Benn Limited, 1962), 61. Whitehead was one of the most perceptive philosophers of the early twentieth century.

35. William James, introduction to Henry James, Sr., *The Literary Remains of Henry James* (Upper Saddle River, N.J.: Literature House, 1970), 118–19.

36. Abraham H. Maslow, *Religion, Values, and Peak-Experiences* (Columbus: Ohio State University Press, 1964). On William James's own experience see Henry James (ed.), *The Letters of William James* (Boston: Atlantic Monthly Press, 1920), I, 95–97, 145–48, 169–71, 199–200, II, 76–77, 211–15, and William James, *Collected Essays and Reviews* (New York: Longmans, Green and Company, 1920), 504–10. See also Gay Wilson Allen, *William James: A Biography* (New York: Viking Press, 1967), and Ralph Barton Perry, *The*

critic of James, said that James represented "the true
America." That assessment seems correct on two scores:
(1) The active will and, hence, the active virtues played a
decisive role in James's own hold on selfhood, and (2)
James both benefited from and supported the American
moral system. Santayana also pointed out that, while
James was skeptical and questioning in his approach to
science, he was much less so in morals.[37] Like his fellow
Americans, then, he clung to an active selfhood, a conventional morality, and an accepted patriotism.

So long as God lived, whether above or within the
evolutionary process, and all seemed to be well with America, moral assurance continued. In fact, American presidents and missionaries sought to export the American
moral system. But when cracks began to appear in the
security of American identity, the moral system began to
give way. As we got deeper into the twentieth century
there were signs of less than the complete triumph of
American idealism abroad and increasingly more urgent
reminders of the depth of uneasiness within American
society itself. The Great Depression struck a blow at the
active virtues. Short-term resuscitation followed when full
mobilization of American energies was required by entry
into the Second World War. But the consequent accelerated technological development further altered the nature of work in America and also further undermined the
work ethic.

The cold war ideology of the late forties and fifties

Thought and Character of William James (2 vols.; Boston: Little,
Brown and Company, 1936). James's views of religious experience
are systematically set forth and illustrated in his *The Varieties of
Religious Experience* (New York: Macmillan, 1961).

37. Santayana, *Character and Opinion in the United States*,
Chap. 3. For a much more sympathetic treatment of James than that
by Santayana or even than what is implied in my own brief treatment, see William A. Clebsch, *American Religious Thought: A History* (Chicago: University of Chicago Press, 1973), Chap. 6.

demanded a renewed confidence in American virtue and uniqueness. But the very juxtaposition of two opposing systems—one unequivocally identified as good and the other as evil—tended to transform the onetime American universalism into a new Manichaean dualism. If the world were irretrievably divided between the forces of light and darkness, then where was the universal, all-powerful deity? If he were on our side, as many confidently proclaimed, then what about the real difficulties we encountered in the hot wars in Korea and Vietnam? The latter of these encounters especially raised the most serious questions in American history regarding the uniqueness and universal significance of the American enterprise.

These questions were exacerbated as consciousness of moral relativity reached a new high. Moral practice, both individual and social, evidenced increasing departure from the accepted American moral system. In sexual relations there was a sharp increase in practices, or in public acceptance of phenomena, once generally regarded as immoral or even illegal: premarital intercourse, adultery, homosexual acts and relationships, birth control, and abortion. In public life, formally acknowledged traditional moral principles thinned to the breaking point as they were stretched to cover up increasingly more serious involvement by public figures in immoral and even illegal acts. "Credibility gap" entered the common speech. Presumed truthful statements became "inoperative." Massive deceit appeared to be practiced at the very center of political power. Thus, while we hoped or assumed that the moral system would hold our society together, the flesh-and-blood moral self had seemingly disappeared from our common life.[38]

On top of all this, latter-day rumors of the death of God

38. Wylie Sypher's perceptive statement about a slightly different context is quite appropriate to the recent dramatic evidence of

were perhaps just suggestive enough to raise the volume of anxiety and uncertainty to an unbearable pitch. If God were dead, what was to become of the country and its God-sanctioned moral system? And what now was to become of the surety of the promise of the New World soul? One dictionary definition of *crisis* is "a psychological or social condition characterized by unusual instability caused by excessive stress and either endangering or felt to endanger the continuity of the individual or his group." [39] This is where we are now. We know the threat of division in the body politic; even more significantly, we experience what Arnold Toynbee called a "schism in the soul."[40] We want desperately to put our nation and ourselves back together. We long for the sense of newness, excitement, and promised wholeness of which our fathers seemed so confident.

Americans are experiencing a severe crisis in self-perception and self-confidence. Integrating and energizing experience seems in short supply. Assurance in faith and morals has slipped away. Religious institutions and traditions have become spiritual straitjackets for many and almost totally irrelevant enterprises for others. The destiny and priorities of the nation are severely questioned.

This crisis and its effects are especially evident among the young. Sensitive young people manifest a sense of loss and a near despair that is only slightly tempered by a poignant hope to find a sense of direction. Clearly the hope, confidence, and idealism of earlier American self-perception, if it could now be appropriated by the youth,

---

moral deterioration: "We are continually destroying the moral self while we keep hoping that our old moral contrivances can hold our organizations together." *Loss of the Self in Modern Literature and Art* (New York: Random House, 1962), 14.

39. *Webster's Third New International Dictionary.*

40. Arnold Toynbee, *A Study of History* (London: Oxford University Press, 1934–61), V, 376–568.

would move over this land like a cleansing flow of fresh air. But such self-perception seems to be beyond secure claim. In discussing this current crisis, especially among youth, anthropologist Margaret Mead asserts that we are experiencing "a crisis in faith, in which men, having lost their faith not only in religion, but also in political ideology and in science, feel they have been deprived of every kind of security. . . . [This situation] can be attributed, at least in part, to the fact that there are now no elders who know more than the young themselves about what the young are experiencing. . . . Today the elders can no longer present with certainty moral imperatives to the young." Dr. Mead illustrates her position with the following words from a fifteen-year-old Texas boy:

> There is a mass confusion in the minds of my generation in trying to find a solution for ourselves and the world around us.
> We see the world as a huge rumble as it swiftly goes by with wars, poverty, prejudice, and the lack of understanding among people and nations.
> Then we stop and think: there must be a better way and we have to find it.
> We need a great deal of love for everyone, we need a universal understanding among people, we need to think of ourselves and to express our feelings, but that is not all. I have yet to discover what else we need. . . .
> Sometimes I walk down a deserted beach listening to the waves and birds and I hear them forever calling and forever crying. . . . The answer is out there somewhere. We need to search for it.[41]

This boy had not yet reached the brink of despair. Other youths reached that brink—and went over it. Here, for example, are the words of a onetime editor of the Harvard *Crimson* who received his B.A. degree in 1968: "Many people of my [college] generation had very little faith in

41. Margaret Mead, *Culture and Commitment: A Study of the Generation Gap* (Garden City, N.Y.: Natural History Press, 1970), 81–82, 76.

themselves. Many were afraid that in coming to grips with
the real world, they would in fact become what they
despised."[42]

Some elders might protest that it is natural for youth to
question. But is it possible that the quality and range of
the questioning by today's youth are different, that there
is something in the context of this agonized groping that is
new? There is now, for example, the possibility of universal death, which first invaded human consciousness at
Hiroshima and has more recently been exacerbated by a
rising awareness of an environmental crisis that threatens
to deplete the earth's life-sustaining resources or to inun-
date the human race in its own pollution. Earlier Americans could, at the least, find immortality in their posterity.
Now even "posterity" has become a large question mark.
And for American youth the situation is confounded by
the fact that it was the United States that dropped the
atomic bomb, that sent the harbinger of a possible universal death. It is also the United States that is the world's
greatest consumer of the earth's resources and one of its
greatest polluters. It is ironic, to put it mildly, that the
apostle of a newborn soul is also apparently the messenger
of mass death.

An Arunta tribe of Australia, the Achilpa, revered a
sacred pole that symbolized their access to meaning and
life. According to Achilpa mythology, the god who had
called the tribe into existence had used this pole to de-
scend from and ascend to the upper realms. At one critical
juncture in the life of the tribe the pole was broken. The
tribe was so disoriented by this experience that it became
immobilized and finally died.[43] Have the meaningful concepts, models, and sanctities of *our* common life become

42. Los Angeles *Times*, March 30, 1973.
43. On the Achilpa see Mircea Eliade, *The Sacred and the Profane: The Nature of Religion* (New York: Harper and Row, 1961),
33.

so disarrayed and destroyed that all we have left in common is death? Few cultures have avoided the subject of death as much as ours, and yet none has matched ours in the potency of its powers of death. The Achilpa died because they could not change. Do we face the same fate? Or can we change?

RENEWED SEARCH

It may not be surprising that in the present situation we are experiencing in America an unparalleled spiritual ferment. This is not to say that organized religion is growing, either in numbers or in spiritual strength. But it is to say that people are almost desperately seeking life and ways of affirming life against the threat of death, security against the threat of chaos, probity against the threat of complete moral anarchy, hope against the threat of despair, and wholeness to heal the schism in their souls.

The depth of our crisis is evident in the primal character of the current individual and communal search for soul. Valid and validating experience is sought. Through encounter group or spirit possession or magical formula or chemical means or religious conversion or transcendental meditation, people seek to probe the depths of the human psyche in order to release the vital powers hidden there, to get in touch with the collective unconscious, to experience God, or to become attuned to cosmic consciousness. Others strive vigorously to reappropriate the power of a communal soul—black, Chicano, native American, or Jewish. Some, in a remarkable replication of an earlier romantic mood, long to get back to the garden, to that land and time and community where the slate is wiped clean and all things are made new. Increasing numbers look to Asian religious traditions for the energizing formulas that will help them to achieve a fulfillment at once intensely personal and cosmically significant. Still others seek to revivify the certainties of American faith and morals and of "that old-time religion," which supported these certainties.[44]

Focus on two sharply contrasting moods, outlooks, and styles may help to illustrate the broad range and the significance for America of this current search for soul. On the one side are the staunch defenders of traditional American beliefs and morals, on the other are their deniers; on the one hand are those who see American technological civilization with its religious tradition as the way to salvation, on the other hand are those who see that civilization as leading only to damnation and disintegration. If we were to symbolize these contrasting moods, an appropriate symbol of the former might be a rocket ship and, of the latter, a flower.

The *rocket ship* is one of the most dramatic symbols in human history. Not only does its creation involve the extraordinary bringing together of impressive and complex forces; its actual launching represents the apparent fulfill-

44. There is a large literature on the religious and spiritual ferment of our time. For a systematic treatment of recent developments see James M. Gustafson (ed.), "The Sixties: Radical Change in American Religion," *Annals of the American Academy of Political and Social Science*, No. 387 (January, 1970). I have also found the following useful: Robert S. Ellwood, *One Way: The Jesus Movement and Its Meaning* (Englewood Cliffs, N.J.: Prentice-Hall, 1973), and Erling Jorstad, *That New Time Religion: The Jesus Revival in America* (Minneapolis: Augsburg Publishing House, 1972), on the so-called Jesus movement; Richard Quebedeaux, *The Young Evangelicals* (New York: Harper and Row, 1974), on developments in Protestant evangelicalism; Robert S. Ellwood, *Religious and Spiritual Groups in America* (Englewood Cliffs, N.J.: Prentice-Hall, 1973), and Jacob Needleman, *The New Religions* (Garden City, N.Y.: Doubleday, 1970), on what Needleman calls "the new religions" and Ellwood refers to as the "alternative reality" tradition; and Theodore Roszak, *The Making of a Counter Culture* (Garden City, N.Y.: Doubleday, 1969) and *Where the Wasteland Ends: Politics and Transcendence in Postindustrial Society* (Garden City, N.Y.: Doubleday, 1972), and George B. Leonard, *The Transformation: A Guide to the Inevitable Changes in Humankind* (New York: Delacourte Press, 1972), on the current primal search for renewing experience.

ment of a recurring dream and aspiration to escape the confines of the earth. Those who viewed on television the launch of Apollo 17, the last of the series of moon missions, may recall that due to a last-minute malfunction there was a considerable delay before the rocket ship lifted from its launching pad. During this delay, television cameras focused repeatedly on that long, sleek, tapered instrument, sitting there, pointed into the night sky, vapors playing about its base, attendant paraphernalia loyally supplicating with uplifted arms. It was as if we viewers were witnessing some primeval enactment, fit for the gods themselves. And yet it was very modern and very American. Here was the spaceship *America* about to be thrust into outer space, carrying its mission to the moon, the final effort in the series that President Richard Nixon, on the successful completion of one of the earlier missions, had called the most significant event since the creation itself.

This active, heroic approach is of a piece with the energetic and hopeful spirit that led to the discovery, exploration, and settlement of America. It represents a continuous and confident quest to master nature, to show, in the words of astronaut Eugene Cernan, that "nothing is impossible in this world if dedicated people are involved." At the same time this spirit, which the Greeks might have called *hubris*, continues to be allied with divinity. Americans and God work together in taking mankind "into a new era."[45]

Here, then, is a continuing wedding of religiosity and American enterprise typical of the American ethos in the past century. Will it carry the day? Will spiritual awareness and sensitivity match the colossal technical feat of the moon mission? Clearly everyone from the astronauts to the president wished it to be a positive, life-affirming

45. Santa Barbara *News Press*, December 19, 1972, Los Angeles *Times*, December 20, 1972.

experience. And one could hardly help but feel a sense of awe, a thrill of power, and perhaps even a touch of self-assurance in witnessing the drama of the moon mission. One hopes that it might revitalize the human spirit and reinvigorate our civilization. Still, one remembers sadly that rockets are also used to destroy. And one notes a striking resemblance in shape among a rocket, a guided missile, a nuclear bomb, and a supersonic bomber. This symbol speaks of both life and death.

The *flower* symbolizes naturalness, earthiness, simplicity, beauty, and fertility. It says: Do what comes naturally; shake off your societal hang-ups. It invites us to reenter Mother Nature's womb. It would give up all effort to master or to change nature. Those who offer the flower are, consciously or unconsciously, radical critics of American civilization—and, for that matter, of any civilization. For vital paradigms they turn to nature and to those primitive cultures that are presumed to be closest to nature. We have seen in our time a remarkable resurgence of this romantic mood. It assumes, like Jean Jacques Rousseau, that man was born free and is everywhere in chains. Let him throw off his chains by shedding all those phony accretions of civilized life. Let him respond not to his head, but to his guts. That is where he really lives. The ideal is not Apollo but Dionysus.

These two contrasting approaches are reminiscent of Toynbee's description of two sharply opposite reactions to "the disintegration of civilizations":

> The passive attempt consists in an *abandon* . . . in which the soul 'lets itself go' in the belief that, by giving free reign to its own spontaneous appetites and aversions, it will be 'living according to nature' and will automatically receive back from that mysterious goddess the precious gift of creativity which it has been conscious of losing. The active alternative is an effort at self-control . . . in which the soul 'takes itself in hand' and seeks to discipline its 'natural passions' in the opposite belief that nature is the bane of

creativity and not its source and that to 'gain mastery over nature' is the only way of recovering the lost creative faculty.[46]

There are many between these opposite poles who seek to change society, who wish to recover "the lost creative faculty," but who do not want to throw off all civilization. They understand that complete abandon to whim is a spiritual dead end. It fails to acknowledge, as critic George B. Leonard notes, that "everyone of us was born in civilization" and that spiritual renewal must deal with man as both an individual and a social being. "A classic case of an experiment which completely ignored this problem," Leonard points out, "which indeed tried every shortcut towards pleasure, is that of the hippie movement which arose in the mid-1960's."[47]

On the other hand, merely to reaffirm the old ways seems also to be a spiritual cul-de-sac. The advanced technology and heroic activism of the space age are not matched by an equally advanced spirituality. "What can we gain by sailing to the moon," asked the late Thomas Merton, "if we are not able to cross the abyss that separates us from ourselves?"[48] Growth and change are required in the spiritual realm too, and that requires thought, discipline, experimentation, and commitment.

Today on a hundred different fronts men and women are experimenting with new means in their search for soul. The experiments that will probably prove most long lasting in influence will be those that can, on the one hand, stimulate or elicit the power of spiritually transforming experience and faith and, on the other hand, channel that power into disciplined action. What is needed is a combina-

46. Arnold Toynbee, *A Study of History* (Abridged ed.; New York: Oxford University Press, 1947), I, 429.

47. Leonard, *The Transformation*, 229.

48. Thomas Merton, *The Wisdom of the Desert Fathers* (New York: New Directions, 1960), 11.

tion that holds in creative tension a number of seeming
opposites: spontaneity and control, spirituality and practi-
cality, ecstacy and action, grace and morality, virtue and
power, individuality and community. This kind of combination has not been common in American history in the
past century. American spirituality has tended to become
flat, one-dimensional, and hence out of touch with deeper
sources of self-perception and spiritual power. But, as is
suggested in chapters three and four, America is neither
totally lacking in spiritual resources nor wholly deficient in
affording that kind of context conducive to spiritual experimentation and even the development of spiritual
strength.

To what extent can the earlier vision of the New World
soul be reappropriated into the current individual and
communal quest for soul? And to what extent will Americans have to look elsewhere for vitalizing visions that will
give meaning and power to their lives? Indeed, is the very
notion of the newborn soul in this new land any longer
appropriate or realistic? Perhaps, in fact, the claim to
newness, uniqueness, and universality was all along a naïve,
overly optimistic, and finally even self-defeating claim.
Whatever the case, it is clear that the search for a *uniquely
American* soul has been, as suggested in the next chapter,
an elusive and difficult quest, and it still goes on.

2

Separation and the Search
for an American Soul

America is "a land of separated men."—Oscar Handlin

"Our ancestors sought a new continent. . . . What they found was a new condition of mind."—James Russell Lowell

"Home is found nowhere. . . . I now love only my children's land, yet undiscovered."—Friedrich Nietzsche

In one of his more recent efforts to describe the American scene, the journalistic social analyst Vance Packard announced somewhat gloomily that we have become "a nation of strangers."[1] Impressive evidence supports this conclusion. At least one family in five moves each year. Neighborhood, community, and family ties are strained and frequently broken. This mass mobility exacts a heavy human toll. Mobility, however, is not new in America. We are a nation of immigrants and migrants. The family of Ethan Allen was "like the Israelites," according to one of his biographers. "They raised families and moved. Four generations averaged ten children each and lived in eight different places."[2] Much of the American story can be written in terms of means of locomotion—from the horse to the jet airplane and the covered wagon to the modern moving van.

Mobility may, in fact, be built into American self-percep-

1. Vance Packard, *A Nation of Strangers* (New York: McKay, 1972).
2. John Pell, *Ethan Allen* (London: Constable and Company, 1929), 2.

tion. "America is a utopia," said Alfonso Reyes, the Mexican statesman. "It is the name of a human hope."[3] This "nowhere," this open future, invites movement, invites one to leave home, to take a trip. Hence America became, in the words used by Oscar Handlin in his classic study of immigration, a "land of separated men."[4] Here one discovered what it meant to be an individual apart from place or people. Here apparently it was possible to engage in a new kind of search for self-realization. But that individuality and that search depended on openness, on the possibility of movement in space and time.

Mobility is, of course, not new to the human race, as mention of the Israelites (or any nomadic tribe) may remind us. What was new in the American context was not mobility itself, although American technology has undoubtedly accelerated mobility, but the relative absence of a communally based and traditionally sacralized sense of self or soul. The Israelites moved, but with a divinely sanctioned sense of peoplehood and destination. They were the chosen people bound for the promised land. This gave their mobility direction and purpose. The separated American could not easily rely, however, on such a sure sense of peoplehood to give direction to his mobility. With neither a clear destination nor a pillar of fire to guide, mobility in America could mean rootlessness, homelessness, loneliness, and despair as well as challenge, openness, and excitement.

INDIVIDUALISM VERSUS
THE SEARCH FOR PEOPLEHOOD

One dictionary definition of *people* is "a body of persons composing a community, tribe, race or na-

3. Quoted in F. S. C. Northrop, *The Meeting of East and West: An Inquiry Concerning World Understanding* (New York: Macmillan Company, 1946), 66.
4. Oscar Handlin, *The Uprooted* (New York: Grosset and Dunlap, 1951), 305.

tion . . . sometimes viewed as a unity."[5] Obviously people-hood, so understood, has been of great importance in human history. Psychologically, the sense of being a part of a people has played a large and often dominant role in human self-understanding. Children are born into and shaped by community—common language, symbols, practices, and concepts. Community may even be sacralized—*i.e.*, given a sense of ultimate meaning and purpose—by reference to acts of god or gods. These acts, and the memory of them, are often associated with a special time and place, which in turn become holy. Separation from this sacred cosmos is painful unless the god can also travel. A mobile ark of the covenant or mobile deities may help to preserve a sense of unity and direction among a mobile people.

It is not clear, however, whether even a mobile ark has been possible in America. A common sense of peoplehood has not been easily achieved. First, deep sectional differences had to be surmounted before the ideal of "one nation indivisible" could be approached, and that required a Civil War, which inflicted deep wounds. Then the very notion of the New World soul, which was premised on a necessary departure from one's past, was most often couched in highly individualistic terms not conducive to communal depth. Finally, from the beginning America has been a "nation of nations," a land of many peoples, and the achievement of an inclusive, satisfactory, and viable sense and image of peoplehood has been extraordinarily difficult. *E pluribus unum* has remained an unattained ideal.

Without discussing further the matter of sectional differences, let us turn first to the phenomenon of American individualism and its effects. There seems to have occurred in America the culmination of that long process of separation from all that is sacred, a process sometimes called

5. *Compact Edition of the Oxford English Dictionary.*

secularization. America was the place where new, modern notions of selfhood could be tested. Most of these notions put much confidence into the emergence of the individual as a competent, self-reliant, rational, and free entity, whose strength sprang directly from nature or the reason or the will, not from place or people or even the gods. Such a person could make it regardless or even in spite of heritage and without any of the perquisites of special privilege.[6]

The image of the free individual was exhilarating no doubt. But the resulting independence or self-dependence put a heavy burden on the individual and on whatever provisional community he might develop. Separation from place, people, and deity could entail both freedom and loneliness, release and alienation, spiritual enthusiasm and spiritual hollowness. The "fractions of my heritage," reflected novelist Vance Bourjaily in his *Confessions of a Spent Youth*, "were merely that, fractions, adding up to no Englishman, Welshman, or Arab, so that for me, as for many, there is no heritage. Each of us is a fresh, slightly different combination." Each is an individual, a separated self, a "fractional man," to use Bourjaily's designation. Encountering his Arab relatives during the Second World War, Bourjaily found himself to be "uselessly complicated and discontent as they were simple and steadfast and proud."[7]

The virgin land invited the resourceful individual to settle, develop, exploit. This could command his full energies and result in an absorption in work akin to religious

6. On the separated, rationalized individual see A. M. Schlesinger, Sr., "The American—A New Man," in Oscar Handlin (ed.), *Children of the Uprooted* (New York: G. Brazziller, 1966), 193–216, and Yehoshua Arieli, *Individualism and Nationalism in American Ideology* (Cambridge: Harvard University Press, 1964).

7. Vance Bourjaily, *Confessions of a Spent Youth: A Novel* (New York: Dial Press, 1960), 273; see also Handlin (ed.), *Children of the Uprooted*, 474.

fulfillment. But space, land, and the goods of this world often became consuming passions for Americans. Little time was to be had for reflection and for the spiritual discipline that could bring human depth. The self that emerged under these circumstances tended to be restless and constantly in search of new worlds to conquer. Long after the close of the land frontier, space surrogates had to be found in "new frontiers" or in the "space race" or in the recesses of the mind itself. The imagination must be continually stoked, the future must always be open, and there must be space in which to move; without these the separated self might loose its life-giving sustenance.

Historically, there has been a strong thrust in this country toward separation from people and place. This has put a heavy burden on the nuclear family and, at the same time, a premium on the early achievement of independence. In America, as Tocqueville observed, the family does not exist in the conventional sense.[8] Prolonged and sustained nurture, typical of tribal, archaic, and aristocratic cultures, was not possible here. Early maturity was forced; in a sense, every child was born a man. This is evident in both folklore and religion. John Henry, a hero of folk song and saga, was born a full-grown and powerful man. The elder Henry James complained bitterly about the early spiritual maturity that his father's Calvinism apparently demanded of him in his childhood.[9]

The American mother faced an enormous task of acculturating her children on the run and often without help from husband or other family members. "American moth-

8. For the Tocqueville reference and for a larger treatment of the subject, see Arthur W. Calhoun, *A Social History of the American Family from Colonial Times to the Present* (3 vols.; Cleveland: Arthur H. Clark Company, 1918–19), esp. II, 53, and Oscar and Mary F. Handlin, *Facing Life: Youth and the Family in American History* (Boston: Little, Brown and Company, 1971).
9. Henry James, Sr., *The Literary Remains of Henry James* (Upper Saddle River, N.J.: Literature House, 1970), 160.

ers," as Erik Erikson has observed, "stepped into the role of the grandfathers as the fathers abdicated their dominant place in the family, in the field of education, and cultural life. The post-revolutionary descendants of the Founding Fathers forced their women to be mothers *and* fathers, while they continued to cultivate the role of freeborn sons."[10] In the process the mother tended to become purposive in an overly direct and not obviously affectionate way. The child, separated from the nest early, developed a peculiar emotional dependency and guilt generally covered over by a brave exterior. This emotion was often expressed in American folk songs and tales, in which there appeared side by side themes of heroic adventure and of restlessness and loneliness. It was dangerous to be overly demonstrative in love; there was so little duration and substance in human relationships. "Apparently these people who weren't afraid of Indians, or loneliness, or the varmints, or the woods, or freedom, or wild horses, or prairie fires, or drought, or six-guns," observed the Lomaxes in their treatment of folk songs, "were afraid of love."[11]

In this world, home was an evasive and poignant symbol. Perhaps it was the fleeting and yet idolized mother's love. "Lost sinners" were beseeched to "come home"—to that mother's love and to the evangelical religion and morality that she had so arduously urged and upheld. What Thomas Oden calls "the intensive group experience,"[12] which was characteristic of pietistic Protestantism—as in the Wesleyan class meetings, for example—provided an emotional home or way station for some. This was a kind of surrogate extended family or ethnic group. But, in the mobile American society, home remained a fluid notion. It was ahead,

10. Erik Erikson, *Childhood and Society* (Middlesex, England: Penguin Books, 1965), 287.

11. Quoted *ibid.*, 293.

12. Thomas Oden, *The Intensive Group Experience: The New Pietism* (Philadelphia: Westminster Press, 1972).

over the mountain, around the bend—tomorrow. One could not afford to stop along the way. "Home," said my father, a second-generation American, "is where you hang your hat."

IMMIGRATION AND ITS EFFECTS

Into this land of mobility and individualism came a great flood of immigrants—over thirty million in the period between the Civil War and the First World War. These men and women learned by bitter experience what it meant to be separated. The "history of immigration," says Handlin, "is a history of alienation and its consequences." The very decision to emigrate usually involved an assertion of individuality. That decision was "a momentous one which transformed the emigrant's life." From that moment he "was confronted almost daily" with other decisions for which his previous life in a particular place and as part of a particular people had not prepared him. "Strangers, the immigrants could not locate themselves; they had lost the polestar that gave them their bearings."[13]

In actuality, there appears to have been a double movement within the soul of the immigrant—one toward an assertion of individuality, which tended to cut him off from his anchorage in a traditional society and cast him adrift in the New World, and a countermovement toward reestablishing in the New World as many elements of the old as possible. The decision to leave home set in motion a centrifugal force that tended to war with the centripetal pull of place and people. These warring forces sometimes pulled apart families and even individuals.[14]

In the nature of the case, the immigrant's identity was

13. Handlin, *The Uprooted*, 4–5, 94.
14. For dramatic treatments of the countervailing pulls on the immigrant, see Ole Rölvaag's treatment of the tension between Per Hansa and his wife Beret in *Giants in the Earth* and the inner tensions that led to suicide in the case of Mr. Schmerda in Willa Cather's *My Antonia*.

initially tied to the Old World. Hence he usually sought his own people in the New World and with them established or attempted to establish his own institutions—press, native societies, churches—his own Old World community in the New World. Handlin points out that the first concern of immigrant self-help societies was to deal with the details of death.[15] In the Old World this critical time of passage was securely ritualized. The New World seemed to have little time or place for death, however. Ritualization (and sacralizing) were catch-as-catch-can affairs, put together to assuage a numbing emptiness. Stoyan Christowe, a Bulgarian immigrant, wrote of his own mixed feelings at his father's funeral on the high Great Plains:

> I was thinking how different my mother's funeral had been [in the old country].... The procession here through the treeless plain was unreal and unbelievable. There was something incomplete, unfinal, about my father's death, and about his burial. This was no way to return a man to his eternal resting place. No bell tolled; no priests in vestments swung fuming censers or intoned funeral chants....
> It was a lonely and remote spot, but a more fitting burial place could hardly be found, for scarcely fifty feet away was one of those mesas that rise sheer from the plains, like temples, to heights of two and three hundred feet. No one could be in the shadow of this majestic tableland without being aware of something mysterious and supernatural dwelling within its terraced sides.... That in itself seemed to make up, in some measure, for the lack of religious rites.[16]

Christowe was already considerably advanced along the road that moved him psychologically from the Old World to the new, and from that critical point on he became more and more the new man.

Christowe's experience was not unlike that of a young Italian who recalled with nostalgia the artistic grandeur

15. Handlin, *The Uprooted*, 173.
16. Stoyan Christowe, *My American Pilgrimage* (Boston: Little, Brown and Company, 1947), 241–42.

and great monuments of his Old World culture but then put these behind him in order "to build the future." This required, above all, active work. Work he did, until "it became more pleasure to work than to take leisure. Suddenly," he concluded, "it looks to me like that is the American, that is what the American is always to do, always to work for achievement. It came to me, like I am born—I am American."[17]

The New World call for separation and focus on the future was as great as that uttered by Jesus when he said, "Leave the dead to bury their own dead."[18] This, after all, was the land of the living. Here, as Thomas Jefferson put it, *"the earth belongs in usufruct to the living* [and] the dead have neither power nor rights over it."[19]

MONOLITHIC AMERICANISM

The great flood of immigrants that rolled over American shores in larger and larger numbers up to the First World War was cause for increasing alarm among "old Americans." Many became concerned to "Americanize" these foreigners. But what did it mean to Americanize? Was there a pattern of peoplehood to which these foreigners could be fitted? Was there an *American people* in the sense of the dictionary definition quoted above? Was there a one (*unum*) into which the many (*pluribus*) flowed? To put it another way: Was it possible to become an unhyphenated American?

Two homogenizing concepts of Americanization emerged.[20] One, following the early vision of the New

17. Quoted in Robert E. Park and Herbert A. Miller, *Old World Traits Transplanted* (New York: Harper and Brothers, 1921), 276.

18. Matthew 8:22, Revised Standard Version.

19. Quoted in R. W. B. Lewis, *The American Adam: Innocence, Tragedy, and Tradition in the Nineteenth Century* (Chicago: University of Chicago Press, 1955), 16.

20. Oscar Handlin discusses and gives examples of three concepts of Americanization in Oscar Handlin (ed.), *Immigration as a Factor*

World soul, stressed the newness and uniqueness of a man and a people still aborning. The other urged conformity to an existing pattern—the pattern of the "old American," which was generally understood as that of the white, Anglo-Saxon Protestant. The first concept was put most graphically in the image of the melting pot. From this crucible, which contained representatives of many people, one new people and one new type of man would emerge. But, for such melting-pot praisers as Israel Zangwill, the character of this new people and new self was not yet fully evident: "The real American has not yet arrived."[21]

The second concept of Americanization was based on the presumed superiority of a particular people and their identity with American peoplehood. In this view the melting pot became a transmuting or converting pot, in which aliens and strangers were transformed into Americans—that is, after the likeness of the "old Americans." According to Edmund Traverso, Henry Ford arranged a pageant in the early 1920s to illustrate this idea of Americanization. Ford ordered a large pot constructed outside his factory.

> On the day of the pageant groups of immigrants dressed in the colorful costumes of their native lands, marched and danced [toward the pot].
>
> When the group at the front of the procession reached the enormous pot it sang and danced one final chorus of its song and then disappeared inside. One by one the various groups followed the first.
>
> From the other side of the ... pot there began to emerge people dressed alike in the current American fashion. Forming ranks, they began to sing in clear English, "The Star Spangled Banner." Weaker and weaker grew the refrains of the tarantellas, polkas, and kolos as more and more people emerged from the pot to swell the chorus of the national anthem. At last the foreign tunes and words were heard no more; the final flash of color

in American History (Englewood Cliffs, N.J.: Prentice-Hall, 1959), including, in addition to the two I discuss as "homogenizing concepts," the notion of pluralism.

21. Israel Zangwill, *The Melting-Pot: A Drama in Four Acts* (New York: Macmillan Company, 1911), 38.

disappeared into the pot. All that could now be seen was a mass of people dressed alike and marching together. All that was heard was one song and one language.[22]

Both the melting-pot and the transmuting-pot theorists tended to be culturally and psychologically naïve. They assumed that culture was like a mask, which could be put on and off at will. They were essentially children of the eighteenth-century Enlightenment, which exalted nature over culture, which thought it knew what nature and the natural man were like, and which assumed that little more than an act of will was required to become like that man of nature. This was the same age in which Protestant pietists tended to assume that conversion, as they understood it, was a universal phenomenon that transcended all cultural differences. Any man could be almost instantaneously Christianized.[23] This shallow understanding of human cultural and psychological conditioning quite easily led to a *monolithic Americanism*—the ideal of a single character-type and a culturally and spiritually unified people. It was relatively easy to assume that such an end was both possible and desirable.

The melting-pot theorists at least placed this homogenization in the future. Americanization, affirmed Hartley Burr Alexander in 1919, has "yet to be created."[24] In this fashion, the melting-pot or new-man theorists appealed to

22. Edmund Traverso, *Immigration: A Study in American Values* (Boston: Heath, 1964), 75.

23. Roy Harvey Pearce, *The Savages of America: A Study of the Indian and the Idea of Civilization* (Rev. ed.; Baltimore: Johns Hopkins University Press, 1965), 33. Pearce says with reference to this kind of Protestantism that conversion was everything, civilization nothing. This is overstated. Missionaries were concerned with such ingredients of civilization as language, for example, and they made valiant efforts to teach reading and writing. But they were also relatively unaware of the depth and pervasiveness of the cultural hold on the American natives, or any other peoples, as far as that goes.

24. Hartley Burr Alexander, "Americanization," *Nation*, CIX (September 13, 1919), 367.

the enormously attractive pull of images of newness, hope, and promise.

The radical Americanists, the transmuting-pot theorists, were more ruthless. They stressed, as John Higham points out, "complete identification" with the new nation, an "identification so all-embracing as to permeate and stabilize [the individual's] thinking and behavior."[25] This necessitated, in the words of the superintendent of New York City schools in 1917, the "absolute forgetfulness of all obligations or connections with other countries." [26] This forced lobotomy only produced more "separated men." And the community of the radical Americanist tended to be a collectivity of "separated men" who were allied in opposition to other and presumed lesser peoples. During what Higham calls "the tribal twenties,"[27] which followed the high point of national consciousness in World War I, strict immigration laws were passed in order to keep undesirable aliens out of the country. And constrictive practices continued to be perpetrated upon undesirable groups within.

Monolithic Americanism idealized a one-dimensional man. One of its favorite constructs, the rugged individual, was understood primarily as a man of space but not of time. He was as flat in character as the Great Plains and as rugged in act as the Rocky Mountains. He was action incarnate. He had little time for such human phenomena as philosophical reflection, spiritual contemplation, ritual enactment, or emotional display. With advanced industrialization this "rugged individual" gave way to the "organization man," who had many of the same qualities. The organization replaced the wide world of space as his pri-

25. John Higham, *Strangers in the Land: Patterns of American Nativism* (New York: Atheneum, 1963), 204–205.
26. Quoted in Park and Miller, *Old World Traits Transplanted*, 281.
27. Higham, *Strangers in the Land*, Chap. 10.

mary arena of activity. And the organization man was also
flat in character, being as routinized as the organizational
bureaucracy itself. He too was activity incarnate, but for
the organization. His goals were the same as those of the
organization, which were the same as those of the nation.[28]

Neither of these types was fitted for either love or
tragedy, for deep involvement in human affairs, for the
fatal flaw of *hubris*, or for a passionate coping with defeat.
The rugged individual might be heroic, but he was so in an
uninvolved and passionless way, like some man from outer
space. Herman Melville's brooding Captain Ahab in *Moby
Dick* was not a typical rugged individual. He was too
involved. The Horatio Alger and William M. Thayer stories
of the late nineteenth century more clearly reveal the
type—in caricature, perhaps, but the flatness of the one-
dimensional man is conducive to caricature. Arthur Miller's
Willy Loman in *Death of a Salesman* is the one-
dimensional man, the separated self, at the end of the line.
In failure he grasps desperately at the accepted symbols of
newness and action to bolster his deflated self. But the
symbols, like the man himself, are hollow. And Willy is
more pathetic than tragic.

Separation could give life to the individual by cutting
him loose from old restrictions and setting him in the
midst of the challenges of the New World. But the resul-
tant situation might flatten the self, pressing it into a
single-purpose type, squeezing out the richness that might
have gone with being part of an ancient culture or a
distinctive people or a traditional religion. Many immigrants experienced this pressure; some succumbed easily
and some resisted. One reported experiencing "a fading of
emotional tones" and "a decided shift from emotional to

28. See Herbert Hoover, *American Individualism* (Garden City,
N.Y.: Doubleday, Page and Company, 1922), and William H. Whyte,
The Organization Man (Garden City, N.Y.: Doubleday, 1956).

rational motives." He "forgot for some years that birds sing, flowers have odor, stars shine." And he did not think of what he liked or disliked, "but of what was advantageous or disadvantageous." Another new American sadly observed, "We are submerged beneath a conquest so complete that the very name of us means something not ourselves." In a striking identification with native Americans he concluded, "I feel as I should think an Indian might feel in the face of ourselves that were."[29] Marcus Lee Hansen, who dealt perceptively with the nature and effects of this monolithic Americanism, points out that for the immigrant the process of becoming Americanized was "often nothing but a treaty of peace with society." Still, some immigrants freely "converted" or attempted to convert. In the process they tended to become more Yankee— *i.e.*, more rationalized—than the native Yankee himself. Hansen also indicates that Americanization forced the second generation to give up or to disavow those relationships with the Old World culture that might have contributed substantially to the achievement of depth in the American soul.[30] Even a selective maintenance of old ways was difficult.

Some nonimmigrant Americans also resisted the homogenizing pressures of monolithic Americanism and found real values in the variety of immigrant cultures. The caustic critic of unquestioning patriotism during the First World War, Randolph S. Bourne, praised the resistant minorities for "keeping us from being swept into a terrible national engine."[31] The "most creative spirits in the United States

29. Quoted in Park and Miller, *Old World Traits Transplanted,* 54–55, and in Horace M. Kallen, "Democracy versus the Melting-Pot," *Nation,* C(February 18, 1915), 194.
30. Marcus Lee Hansen, "The Third Generation," in Handlin (ed.), *Children of the Uprooted,* 259.
31. Randolph S. Bourne, "The Jew and Trans-National America," *War and the Intellectuals: Collected Essays, 1915–1919,* ed. Carl Resek (New York: Harper and Row, 1964), 125–26.

were attracted," remarked Handlin, "by the immigrants whose 'warm, pagan blood' flowed rich by contrast with the austerity about them."[32] But pressure toward homogeneity of selfhood was relentless, and native and minority cultures were either destroyed or submerged.

The public school was generally looked to as the primary institution of Americanization. One of its chief functions was to make converts out of immigrants and true believers out of birthright Americans. Through the public school, monolithic Americanists sought to substitute their understanding of the national community for local, ethnic, and religious communities that had previously been prime movers in education. At the same time, the progressive educators sought to replace uncritical Americanism with a more critical outlook and the WASP image with that of a new, modern, secularized man and community. A new community was to be built within the school. This community, the progressives hoped, would have pervasive effects in society at large. But the progressives, like the radical Americanists, tended to be culturally naïve and monolithic. They thought authentic community could be built anew in the public school, with little regard for family, ethnic, or religious conditioning. They also objected to communal variety, especially of a religious sort, and they vigorously opposed private and parochial schools as being divisive.[33]

This flattening, homogenizing effect of the public school was increased under the impact on educational theory and

32. Henry Steele Commager (ed.), *Immigration and American History: Essays in Honor of Theodore G. Blegen* (Minneapolis: University of Minnesota Press, 1961), 23.

33. On the Americanizing role of the public school, see Robert Michaelsen, *Piety in the Public School: Trends and Issues in the Relationship Between Religion and the Public School in the United States* (New York: Macmillan Company, 1970). On progressive education see the same source and Richard Hofstadter, *Anti-Intellectualism in American Life* (New York: Knopf, 1963), Chap. 14.

practice of a kind of scientism or positivism that tended to
reduce man to a machine and to look down on human
ritual, belief, myth, and symbol as primitive or premodern
manifestations. Human progress was understood in terms
of advancement from superstition and blind faith to rational enlightenment and control. Science was revered as
the means of access to the whole truth about God, man,
and nature. Art was, at best, an entertainment; religion was
merely a primitive survival.

RESURGENT GROUP CONSCIOUSNESS

Monolithic Americanism, especially of the transmuting-
pot variety, has failed. The drive toward standardization in
American society appears to be less forceful today than it
was in Henry Ford's heyday. Traditional individualism and
narrow nationalism seem to be questioned as never before.
And Americans seem to be embarked upon an unprecedented quest for a kind of self-realization that affords
greater depth and viability than the earlier forms of rugged
individualism or narrow nationalism allowed. Much of this
quest is communally oriented. Ethnic self-consciousness
has been on the rise. And Americans without obvious
ethnic roots have endeavored to find viable selfhood or
self-realization in various types of provisional and inten-
tional communities and groups.[34]

Recent developments in education, for example, are
symptomatic of this rising group consciousness. The stan-
dardizing role and effect of the public school have been
subjected to severe critique from various quarters. Even
compulsory education, once a standard item in the Ameri-

34. On renewed communalism and renewed desire for association
see Philip E. Slater, *The Pursuit of Loneliness: American Culture at
the Breaking Point* (Boston: Beacon Press, 1970); Michael Novak,
*The Rise of the Unmeltable Ethnics: Politics and Culture in the
Seventies* (New York: Macmillan Company, 1972); Keith Melville,
Communes in the Counter Culture: Origins, Theories, Styles of Life
(New York: Morrow, 1972); and T. R. Young, *New Sources of Self*
(New York: Pergamon Press, 1972).

can ethos, has been openly questioned.[35] Public schools have also been sharply criticized for their inadequacies or downright failures in dealing with ethnic minorities. For example, in the conclusion to their study of formal education among the Sioux Indians, three scholars point out the similarities in problems and deficiencies between urban ghetto and reservation schools.[36] Educators in both settings "are isolated from the cultural and social milieux of their pupils. . . . Knowing little of their pupils' life, and terrified or appalled by what they do discover, they justify their avoidance with a 'vacuum ideology' of cultural deficiency and deprivation which ignores or derogates the values and knowledge that the pupils have acquired in their own homes and neighborhoods. Meanwhile, the educators preach morals and manners that are vacuous or fatuous given the realities of the domestic lives of the children." The American system, these scholars conclude, goes too far in requiring "the schools to be ethnic melting-pots and ladders of social mobility."

This sort of critique of public education shows a renewed sensitivity to the importance of ethnic and communal factors in identity and self-perception. That sensitivity is also evident in increased advocacy of a formal education that is either attentive to such factors in a larger whole, as in a public-school setting, or is actually controlled by the ethnic community itself. In a recently issued report, for example, the American Jewish Committee task force on the future of the Jewish community in America called for "a movement toward the development of a Jewish school system in the United States."[37] Dedicated

35. For radical critiques of the public schools and of educational institutions generally, see the works of Edgar Z. Friedenberg and Ivan Illich.

36. Murray L. Wax, Rosalie H. Wax, and Robert V. Dumont, *Formal Education in an American Indian Community* (Atlanta: Emory University Press, 1964), 114–15.

37. *The Future of the Jewish Community in America* (New York: American Jewish Committee, 1972), 40.

blacks, Chicanos, and American Indians, highly critical of traditional public-school efforts, have sought to develop communally valid forms of education through local schools, neighborhood centers, and tribal councils. And new communal movements are engaging in educational experimentation.

BLACK CONSCIOUSNESS

The most forceful, dramatically evident, and influential resurgence of group consciousness in recent times is that which occurred in the black community in the 1960s. The black-consciousness movement also sharply illustrates the inadequacies in the monolithic image of the American soul and the persistent difficulties encountered in the search for soul in America.

The story of black people in America is especially poignant and also diagnostic in throwing light on the quest for selfhood in this land of separated persons. Blacks were separated from their homeland and culture by force, not by their own intentions; they were also denied access to the promised land. America, as W. E. B. Du Bois observed seventy-five years ago, yielded the black man no self-consciousness, but only let "him see himself through the revelation of the other world." Hence a "double-consciousness" emerged, a "twoness." The history of the Afro-American is a history of strife between "two warring ideals," a story of a "longing to attain self-conscious manhood," to "merge his double self into a better and truer self."[38]

The culture that emerged from this strife within the soul of the black American and from the harsh realities of this apparently alien world has been in part a counterculture

38. W. E. B. Du Bois, *The Souls of Black Folk*, first published in 1903; quotations from the opening chapter, "Of Our Spiritual Strivings," as taken from John H. Franklin (ed.), *Three Negro Classics* (New York: Avon Books, 1965), 213–15.

and in part a rich, primal culture in its own right. It has, on
the one hand, exalted even to the point of caricature the
ideals of the WASP world, while, on the other hand, it has
displayed a greater depth and quality of soul than that
world has. Themes of restlessness and mobility have been
set in an ultimate context in the black community. The
"sorrow songs" speak of homelessness, longing, and pain,
but they also affirm homecoming, liberation, and joy.
While the major culture often used religion to buttress the
American moral system and to support a heroic and triumphant activism, black experience gave life to themes of
suffering and salvation, alienation and reconciliation, death
and resurrection. It is as if the black were pushed deeper
and deeper into himself and fashioned there in the crucible
of his own tormented soul a way to integral selfhood
beyond or in spite of or through the very impossibilities of
his own situation. At the same time, the experience of
shared suffering and struggle heightened fellow feeling and
communal identity.

Still, the tension described by Du Bois continued to be
very much a reality for each succeeding generation of
blacks. Liberation must be more than a theological band-
aid applied to a gaping and near-mortal wound. It must be
realized here and now. But how? By stressing the religious
and political values of the major culture at its best or by
proclaiming the uniqueness of black culture? By attempting to bridge a yawning chasm or by affirming the
power *to be* in black nationalism? In his quest for self-consciousness the black has moved between these two poles
described by Du Bois. He has sought, on the one hand, to
enter the white world, to become an integral part of the
white culture, and, on the other, to affirm his blackness.
The first major drive in the twentieth century for improv-
ing the lot of colored people in a white world, initiated by
the National Association for the Advancement of Colored
People, was followed by a vigorous assertion of black

nationalism, which even called for a return to black Africa
by Marcus Garvey. The civil-rights movement of the 1950s
and the early 1960s was followed by the shrill cry of
"black power" in the late 1960s. The tension continues;
but the recent affirmation of black consciousness has
brought renewed awareness—among blacks especially, but
to some extent also among nonblacks—of the soul power
generated and evidenced during the history of the black
community in America.

White Americans have reacted to the recent black affirmation in a variety of ways: with uneasiness, fright, resent-
ment, anger and, yet, with fascination, sympathy, and even
attraction. Black nationalism is a stark reminder of problems inherent in American nationalism. The problem of
black self-consciousness is also an American problem writ
large. White Americans see mirrored in the eyes of black
Americans a division within their own souls. They face not
only the problem of conscience so eloquently described
and thoroughly documented by Gunnar Myrdal a generation ago in *An American Dilemma.* They are also confronted with their own problems of achieving integral
selfhood as separated persons in a fragmented and imper-
sonal society. As comedian Flip Wilson says, "Anyone can
have the blues."

Some nonblacks have vigorously reacted to black affirmation by cultivating their own ethnic roots. Those whose
roots are obvious may be fortunate. Seemingly a clear
identity is available to them. But perhaps they have no
alternative. Such, by and large, seems to be the experience
of the Chicano, the American Indian, and other obvious
minorities. The reaction among other Americans is more
complex perhaps; the "majority" is, in fact, an uneasy
collection of minorities and not itself a "people." Some
whites openly or covertly affirm their own presumed innate superiority to blacks. That at least affords them a
kind of counteridentity. Some rediscover ethnic roots in

Poland or Italy or elsewhere. Black affirmation also has
stimulated a rise in Jewish self-consciousness and, inci-
dentally, in self-consciousness among women (the traditional monolithic WASP image of what it means to be an
American has been primarily a male image). Some whites,
deeply attracted to the black-consciousness movement,
sought to ally themselves with it, thinking that they might
find there a wholeness unattained elsewhere. But they
could not become black, and they were even more sharply
reminded of their own alienation and lack of community.[39]

Renewed communal affirmation and quest suggest the
importance of face-to-face human relationships to human
wholeness, of peoplehood to selfhood. The separated person apparently must return or must discover a new home if
he is to be whole. Certainly Henry Ford's view of the
thoroughly rationalized, one-dimensional American is completely inadequate. Homogenization of the type he desired
can produce only a shallow understanding of life. We may,
on the contrary, even value for their richness and their
human authenticity the various styles and forms of peoplehood that have existed and still exist in this country. We
may also sense that the warmth and humanity of the
extended family, the tribe, the ethnic group, or the inten-

39. There is a burgeoning literature on black history and black
consciousness. Among the works and authors that I have found
helpful, in addition to Du Bois, are: Malcolm X, *The Autobiography
of Malcolm X* (New York: Grove Press, 1964); Martin Luther King,
Jr., *Stride Toward Freedom* (New York: Harper and Brothers,
1958) and *Why We Can't Wait* (New York: Harper and Row, 1963);
William H. Grier and Price M. Cobbs, *Black Rage* (New York:
Grosset and Dunlap, 1968); Edmund David Cronin, *Black Moses:
The Story of Marcus Garvey and the Universal Negro Improvement
Association* (Madison: University of Wisconsin Press, 1968); and the
works of James H. Cone and Joseph R. Washington, Jr. For a
suggestive essay on the attraction of whites to black culture, see
Norman Mailer, *The White Negro* (San Francisco: City Lights Books,
1970).

tional community may be an important resource against
the dehumanizing effects of narrow nationalism and of
technology. The affirmation of and quest for community
are important in our time when a triumphant technology
has accelerated mobility and, paradoxically, has both
brought us together and separated us as never before in
human history. We need the support of other people, of
mutually enhancing primary relationships, and of shared
experiences, concerns, and loyalties.

THE LIMITS OF PEOPLEHOOD

Communalism is not without its own inadequacies, however. Narrow communalism may be stultifying to the individual and especially to spiritual quest. Exclusivistic peoplehood can be divisive and even dangerous in a larger world.
The ethnic group, the tribe, the nation, or some form
of peoplehood may be necessary to human identity,
but in this space age, especially, they are no longer adequate to human fulfillment. Today we, and especially the
young, must put self together in and with "spaceship
earth." Communal experience may be helpful and even
necessary in doing this. But it cannot be a final resting
place. It must finally encourage a viable but open selfhood,
on the one hand, and an ultimate universalism, on the
other.

In other words, let the search go on! Insofar as we can
speak of an *American* soul we must speak finally in terms
of openness and universality. Let America continue to be
"a utopia" then, "the name of a human hope."[40] Let
home itself be a utopia—"nowhere," a land "yet undiscovered," as Nietszche put it.[41] Or, better still, let it be
everywhere. To affirm this kind of ultimate universality in

40. See Northrup, *The Meeting of East and West*, 66.
41. Quoted in Rubem A. Alves, *Tomorrow's Child: Imagination,
Creativity, and the Rebirth of Culture* (New York: Harper and Row,
1972), 181.

any meaningful sense, however, the *individual* soul must first be at home with itself. That finally is a religious task. And this apparently has not been America's long suit. Still, there are resources for spiritual integrity in the American experience that are worth recalling in this time of crisis.

Separation made the search for new and viable forms of identity possible. While the virgin land tempted many to exploitation as a means of self-discovery and while others proclaimed the nation to be both mother and father and sought in turn to force all within a narrowly nationalistic family, the opportunity for meaningful work and patriotic warmth undoubtedly enhanced the lives of many. But separation and the new land also made spiritual ventures possible, and, contrary to prevailing views that America is thoroughly materialistic, there has been in American history a continuing strain of spiritual search, experimentation, and commitment. That strain has been augmented by a form of civil polity that has not made exclusive or ultimate claims and has not required conformity to a homogenized image of the American soul. That polity is still valid, but its survival (or restoration) requires a renewed dedication to the classical notions of civility and citizenship, which the Founding Fathers thought essential to our common public enterprise.

3

Soul Reborn: Puritan Experiential Spirituality and Its Legacy

"The onely suitable adequate ultimate object of the soul of man is god himselfe."—Boston Sermons, 1679

> "Take all away from me
> But leave me ecstacy
> And I am richer then
> Than all my fellow-men."
> —Emily Dickinson

"Just to survive . . . we need a new human nature."
> —George B. Leonard

The crisis in America today is, at bottom, a spiritual crisis. There is a "schism in the soul" of America, and Americans experience a deep need to become unified within their own souls.[1] That is what religion is all about. (One of the definitions of religion is that which binds.) "Dynamic religion," to use Henri Bergson's terminology, is both personally and culturally integrating and generative. It involves a mutually nourishing relationship between vital religious experience and the expression of that experience in thought, in moral and ritualistic action, and in community and between transcendent vision and its embodiment in form and act. As religious experience becomes truncated, religious beliefs and practices and approaches to the moral life tend to become static. "Static religion" may attempt to reproduce vital experience, but the attempt is likely to be abortive. What has been a vital relationship becomes mechanical, overly structured, manipulative, and even repressive. Or, to change the figure, static religion is like a plant without a taproot; it must reestablish that root or

1. Arnold Toynbee, in his *A Study of History* (London: Oxford University Press, 1934–61), V, refers to "the schism in the soul" that has characterized declining civilizations.

die.[2] One way to see our crisis today is to view it as a result of movement from dynamic to static religion. The thought system seems to have gone stale, the symbols seem broken, the myths are beleaguered, the rituals seem empty and uninspired, and the moral system seems unduly narrow and restrictive. Most important, a vital, integrating, and generative experience seems to be lacking.

Is it possible in this situation for one to begin anew? Can the soul be transformed? Can sources of regeneration be tapped to energize a lively selfhood? One that is at home in this world and the next? Alive to the present and open to the future? Morally and spiritually whole without being exclusivistic, self-righteous, or unduly rigoristic? Can such sources be tapped without stultifying reliance on the particularities of peoplehood? Without exclusive reliance on national identity or a conviction of American exceptionalism for final meaning?

Every spiritual salesman in America will have his own sure answers to these questions. What is suggested here, however, is not a pat formula. It is rather a sober invitation to consider or reconsider one of the significant sources of spiritual and moral vitality in the American heritage—Puritan experiential spirituality and its legacy. This invitation is issued with full knowledge that one of the fixed dogmas in the American mind today is the conviction that the Puritans and their offspring are responsible for much that is wrong with American society. I confess, however, to a continuing romance with those much-despised and maligned people and to a view that, at their best, they developed a powerful spirituality and a consequent approach to morality very different from the petty, restrictive moralism that has become their hallmark in popular understanding. That understanding is based largely on a confusion of Puritanism with Victorianism.

2. Henri Bergson, *The Two Sources of Morality and Religion* (New York: Henry Holt and Company, 1935), Chaps. 2, 3.

My admiration of the Puritans is not so consummate, however, as to lead me to assert that Puritan spirituality has been the only valid source of moral and spiritual vitality in America or that it is today even the most significant. There are many others, such as the religion of the Enlightenment, various forms of Catholic and Jewish piety and spirituality, and, more recently, various strands of Asian religious thought and practice, which are not treated here. Furthermore, it is clear that Puritan spirituality could be both constrictive and liberating, and Puritan practice was often narrowly exclusivistic and not at all conducive either to maximum individual spiritual development or to that kind of civil society in which such spirituality may freely grow. In less than a decade after the founding of the most important of the Puritan colonies, Massachusetts Bay, that colony expelled Anne Hutchinson and Roger Williams. Both of these people needed greater soul liberty than allowed by that kind of religious and political Puritanism. Although Williams was Puritan to the core in his understanding of spirituality, he differed sharply with his fellow Puritans on the implications of that spirituality for the religious quest and for such questions as a politically enforced religious uniformity, the relationship between church and state, and the proper functions of a civil state. He brought together in his own outlook a combination of spiritual search and civil commitment, which was not only unique in his time but is still meaningful for ours.

Historically, much of American religion has been experience oriented. In the colonial period both the Puritans and the Quakers, who were their spiritual if not their "kissing" cousins,[3] stressed the centrality of an intense personal experience of transcendence. These movements were pro-

3. On the relationship between Puritans and Quakers, I find persuasive Alan Simpson's statement, "An enterprise which began in the sixteenth century by exhorting men to prepare themselves for a miracle of grace and ended by asserting the presence of the Holy

ducts of a Protestant Christian approach that tended to devalue church and sacraments as means of grace and to stress a more immediate relation to God, through biblical study and personal experience. Spiritual autobiography, a recounting of the trials and triumphs of the soul, was a standard feature of this sort of Protestant religion. This tradition launched a spiritual sensibility that has made a deep imprint on American selfhood. Although its influence appears to have neared an end, this spiritual sensibility still has a double relevance today. On the one hand, some understanding of it helps to illumine our past—and our present. On the other hand, as a type if not in specific content, it may illustrate ways to cope with the problem of achieving a viable, human selfhood today.

THE EXPERIENCE OF SAVING GRACE

Professor Owen C. Watkins points out that the Puritans not only wanted to know the truth, they wanted to *feel* it.[4] Knowledge *about* God's saving grace in Jesus Christ was not enough; one must know that grace in his soul. Without that experience, all was lost. With it, a man was born anew. Vital, saving faith, then, was grounded in experience. In the Puritan view one could not bring about the experience of saving faith through his own efforts; only God could do so. Furthermore, although God had fully manifested his redeeming grace in Jesus Christ, he had not made entirely clear either precisely under what circumstances that experience was to be personally known within one's soul or which individuals would have it and which not. This view, then, gave an uncertain quality to life, a sense of the possibility of fuller personal disclosure or experience yet to come. It also suggested that God's

Spirit in every individual is one movement," in *Puritanism in Old and New England* (Chicago: University of Chicago Press, 1955), 1.

4. Owen C. Watkins, *The Puritan Experience: Studies in Spiritual Autobiography* (New York: Schocken Books, 1972), 5.

redeeming grace might be known at almost any time and under almost any circumstances. Hence even the most ordinary experiences could be enhanced by expectation.

Few systems have put so much weight on personal experience as the Puritan's did. The whole cosmic drama of salvation was reenacted within the soul of the self-conscious Puritan. Each man could be a phoenix. Plummeted first into depths of despair by an acute awareness of his own sin and separation from God, he could be elevated, through an experience of divine grace, to heights of unspeakable joy. This mixture of the seemingly unmixable elements of transcendence and the transient, of grace and nature, was such as to make each man a potential spiritual virtuoso. It set up a tension within the human breast that, while it could crush some men, could elicit from others great sensitivity and creativity.[5]

By stressing the natural indwelling presence of God within each man (called variously the inner light, the God within, and that of God within each man), George Fox and his Quaker followers tended to relieve that inner tension between God and man. But the transformed action expected of the God-filled man was no less heroic than that expected of the more orthodox Puritan, who assumed that the gulf between God and man was greater than Fox pictured it.[6]

A RESPONSIVE ETHIC OF GRACE

The Puritan stress on intense personal experience fostered, at its root, an ethic of grace—that is, an ethic of

5. Among the autobiographical writings that illustrate this point, I suggest "The Autobiography of Thomas Shepard," *Publications of the Colonial Society of Massachusetts*, XXVII (1927–30), 345–400; "John Winthrop's Relation of His Religious Experience," *Winthrop Papers* (Boston: Massachusetts Historical Society, 1943), III, 338–44; and the diary and other personal narratives of Jonathan Edwards.

6. Examples of Quaker spirituality can be found in the journals of George Fox and John Woolman.

unusually high standards, which was understood to flow only from that transforming experience of God's saving grace. The Puritans have generally had a bad press for their approach to morality. But, far from being their primary or even sole concern, as they are frequently understood, morality was a secondary matter to them. As Professor Edmund S. Morgan puts it: In a thousand sermons the Puritans stressed "that religion was *not* morality."[7] It is their unhappy fate, however, that the Puritans have generally been associated primarily with a narrow sex ethic and with the now-infamous work ethic.

No doubt some Puritans were unduly preoccupied with sex. Michael Wigglesworth, dour author of the best-selling *Day of Doom*, was greatly disturbed by his own apparent irregularities. Upon doctor's advice he took a "physick" and got married. He does not seem to have been a model husband![8] But it would not be fair to say that his marriage or even his morbid soul searching were typical. Marriage seems generally to have been understood among Puritans as a common vocation or partnership in and through which to respond to God's grace in this world. And there is considerable evidence of tender relations between faithful spouses.

The Puritans have also been put down for the work ethic with its implied assumption that work is *the* way to meaning and worth in life. But initially the Puritans understood work too as a godly vocation or calling, as a prime way of response to God's grace in this world.[9] "Man's chief end," declares the Westminster Shorter Catechism,

7. Edmund S. Morgan, *The Puritan Family: Religion and Domestic Relations in Seventeenth-Century New England* (Rev. ed.; New York: Harper and Row, 1966), 2; emphasis added.

8. Edmund S. Morgan (ed.), "The Diary of Michael Wigglesworth," *Publications of the Colonial Society of Massachusetts*, XXXV (1942–46), 314, 406.

9. See Robert S. Michaelsen, "Changes in the Puritan Doctrine of Vocation," *New England Quarterly*, XXVI (1953), 315–36.

"is to glorify God, and to enjoy Him forever."[10] One could seek to glorify God in work as well as in worship. The whole moral life was understood, then, as flowing from religious experience and hence was seen in a larger context.

It was Benjamin Franklin who most successfully turned Puritanism over, who turned the Puritan ethic of grace into a "work ethic." Franklin confidently sought to cultivate virtue in this world so that he might be successful, and he was. He essayed to do good, and he did well. It was under Franklin's clever tutelage that work was exalted as *the* way to wealth *and* virtue. One needs only to compare Franklin's autobiography with the autobiographical writing of two of his contemporaries, Jonathan Edwards and John Woolman, or Franklin's *Way to Wealth* with Edwards' *The Nature of True Virtue* and Woolman's *A Plea for the Poor* to get some sense of stark contrast in their approaches to morality. For Edwards, true virtue was universal benevolence or love of being in general. Such an attitude could only flow from true religious affections or a true sense (or sensual awareness) of God's beauty and saving grace. This was an ethic of grace and an almost aesthetic ethic. As such, it was a high standard, not easily achieved.[11]

John Woolman, the spiritually sensitive and influential Quaker, exemplified this ethic of grace in his own life as intensely as any American. In his journal he reports having been conscience stricken as a child after destroying a nest of birds. As a young man he was so disturbed by writing a

10. Prepared by a committee of the Westminster Assembly of Divines in 1648, the Shorter Catechism was widely used among English-speaking Calvinist Protestants.
11. See Jonathan Edwards, *The Nature of True Virtue*, foreward by William K. Frankena (Ann Arbor: University of Michigan Press, 1960). On the aesthetic aspect of Edwards see Roland A. Delattre, *Beauty and Sensibility in the Thought of Jonathan Edwards* (New Haven: Yale University Press, 1968), and William A. Clebsch, *American Religious Thought: A History* (Chicago: University of Chicago Press, 1973), Chap. 2.

bill of sale of a Negro slave that, although his living depended on it, he refused to do so again. On occasion he gently argued with tavern keepers over the sponsorship of bawdy shows that used human beings as means rather than ends. In keeping with that "purity of heart," which is "to will one thing," he refused to wear dyed clothing because the dye was made on slave plantations. Of his experience with "the natives of this land," he wrote that, having for many years felt love in his heart toward them, he was moved to undertake a hazardous, exhausting journey into the wilderness among Indians hostile to the English in order—in a striking reversal of the more typical American rationale for contact with the Indians—"that I might feel and understand their life and the spirit they live in, if haply I might receive some instruction for them."[12]

Woolman, in effect, argued against the work ethic, because it demanded too much of a man's soul, and he launched an impassioned plea for the poor, those exploited and often-neglected denizens of a burgeoning commercial society, because he regarded them as being as much God's creatures as any other human beings. He arrived at these and other moral concerns, positions, testimonies, and witnesses, not primarily out of a commitment to certain rules, regulations, or commandments but primarily as a result of a series of inner promptings, which he regarded as the inward movement of that universal God who made and loves all creatures.

THE SUPPORTING CONTEXT
OF EXPERIENTIAL SPIRITUALITY

The ethic of grace was a model for all "twice-born" men. But it could not be directly inculcated because grace itself could not be humanly imbued. Nevertheless, both Puritan

12. John Woolman, *The Journal of John Woolman and a Plea for the Poor* (John Greenleaf Whittier Text; New York: Corinth Books, 1961), 142.

and Quaker tried to provide a context conducive to the
intense personal experience of grace and the action that
flowed from it. Both attempted to nurture and maintain
dynamic religion. Inevitably they encountered severe difficulties, both because of the problems typically associated
with generational gaps and because of the fundamentally
experiential nature of their spirituality.

Puritan religious experience was initially nurtured by and
expressed in a living religious culture. It was grounded in
what was called "historical faith"—the biblical, Augus-
tinian, Calvinist system—and it was, itself, the cornerstone
of both church and state. But neither the American environment nor Puritan spirituality itself was conducive to a
continuing, vital relationship between religious experience
and communal life. Time, mobility, and diversity were all
threats to communal solidarity. Furthermore, the Puritans
tended to be minimalists in ritual and symbol. No symbol
could resonate with the divine glory; no sacrament could
embody the divine mystery. Emerson said of the spirituality of his aunt Mary Moody that it was "independent of
forms and ceremonies." She conceived herself always
"bound to walk in narrow but exalted paths," which led
"to interminable regions of rapturous and sublime
glory."[13] And she walked in those paths alone.

This is not to suggest that means toward spirituality were
neglected in Puritan and Quaker communities. Each placed
a good deal of emphasis on formal education; the Puritans
are especially well known for their efforts in this area.[14]
But there were clearly limits to the religious usefulness of

13. Edward Waldo Emerson (ed.), *Journals of Ralph Waldo Emerson* (Boston: Houghton Mifflin Company, 1909–14), I, 77–78.
14. On the subjects of the continuing vitality of the regenerative
experience from generation to generation, the treatment of children,
and the question of education, see Morgan, *The Puritan Family;*
Robert Ulich, *A History of Religious Education* (New York: New
York University Press, 1968), especially the sections on the New
England Puritans and the Quakers; Samuel Eliot Morison, *The Intel-*

formal education in a system that finally understood the individual to be in direct relation with God. Formal education might prepare one for such a relationship, but it could not effect that relationship. Formal education could be expected to hold up a high standard of virtue, but it could not assure the motive power for embodying that standard.

The early Quakers understood the primary object of formal education to be one of leading children "to an inward communion with God" and to a life in conformity with his will.[15] As such, formal education was considered to be an extension of the primary concern of the Society of Friends itself, and the techniques used in the meetings for worship and business to encourage sensitivity to the promptings of the spirit tended also to be employed in schools. But there was, of course, no guarantee that these techniques would work or that they would not become merely ends in themselves.

Given the difficulty of the agonizing spirituality to which Puritan leaders like Edward Taylor[16] and Jonathan Edwards aspired, doctrines and especially morals could easily become, among lesser men, ends in themselves. Adults, who as children had had the pressing necessity of the Puritan-style conversion dinned into them, were pleased to escape into morality as the sole test of character. It came to be assumed that morality was something that every reasonable person could understand and most determined people could achieve. Such an assumption led

lectual Life of Colonial New England (2nd ed.; New York: New York University Press, 1956); Walter Joseph Homan, *Children and Quakerism: A Study of the Place of Children in the Theory and Practice of the Society of Friends, Commonly Called Quakers* (New York: Arno Press, 1972); and Howard H. Brinton, *Quaker Education in Theory and Practice* (Wallingford, Pa.: Pendle Hill, 1949).

15. Homan, *Children and Quakerism*, 47.

16. Edward Taylor, 1645?–1729, was the most profound of the New England Puritan poets. His works express a keen spiritual sensibility. See Thomas J. Johnson (ed.), *The Poetical Works of Edward Taylor* (Princeton: Princeton University Press, 1966).

to the conclusion that moral education could be imparted much as one might teach a child to spell. That assumption generally informed most formal attempts at moral education in nineteenth-century America.

EVANGELICAL PROTESTANT SPIRITUALITY

The Puritan stress on experience left a deep imprint on American spirituality. The conversion experience became the primary feature of evangelical Protestantism, that child of Puritan and pietist parents, which reached a vigorous maturity in the United States in the early nineteenth century. In the evangelical understanding of conversion, the individual was typically pictured as alone and naked, poised between heaven and hell, and carrying nothing but the Bible in his hand. The coveted conversion experience could clothe him, bring him into the fellowship of the saved, and send him up the road to heaven—could bring the assurances the Bible promised. A regularized system was developed to produce that experience.[17] This revival system was, in some ways, well fitted to an increasingly mobile American society. At the same time, however, it tended to become shallow religiously, theologically, and culturally. Children were treated like adults and adults like children. Conversion was expected without attention to previous conditioning, cultural context, or supportive reli-

17. On revivalism see William G. McLoughlin, Jr., *Modern Revivalism: Charles Grandison Finney to Billy Graham* (New York: Ronald Press Company, 1959); Bernard A. Weisberger, *They Gathered at the River: The Story of the Great Revivalists and Their Impact upon Religion in America* (Boston: Little, Brown and Company, 1958); and William Warren Sweet, *Revivalism in America: Its Origin, Growth, and Influence* (New York: Abingdon Press, 1944). On the evangelical revival of the early nineteenth century, see also Charles Roy Keller, *The Second Great Awakening in Connecticut* (New York: Archon Books, 1968); Catharine C. Cleveland, *The Great Revival in the West, 1797–1805* (Gloucester, Mass.: Peter Smith, 1959); and Whitney R. Cross, *The Burned-Over District: The Social and Intellectual History of Enthusiastic Religion in Western New York, 1800–1850* (Ithaca: Cornell University Press, 1950).

gious symbol and ritual. What was analogous to an initia-
tory or puberty rite was forced on a youngster without
adequate communal and ritual preparation and repeatedly
urged on an adult without adequate regard for levels of
maturity and other means of spiritual growth.

The leading Protestant evangelist of the national period,
Charles G. Finney, became a master at effecting conversions. He did more than any American before Dwight L.
Moody to perfect the revival system. But Finney became
concerned not only to effect conversion but also to maintain its intensity in the convert's continuing spiritual and
moral life. Growing increasingly aware of the relative lack
of continuity and staying power in the revival system,
Finney took steps designed to correct this weakness. He
developed a perfectionist theology, which stressed continuing spiritual and moral growth beyond conversion, and he
became a prime mover in encouraging a number of benevolent, educational, humanitarian, and moral enterprises into
which the convert could direct his new-found energy.[18]

Finney did not extend perfectionist theology as far as
did John Humphrey Noyes, the founder of the Oneida
Community. The most marked, early religious influence on
Noyes was a conversion experience stimulated by a Fin-
ney-type revival. From there Noyes went "on to perfection"—that is, he assumed, on both experiential and theological grounds, that he was without sin and that he and
his like-minded fellows could live in this world in perfect
love. With Noyes, then, the gulf between God and man,
nature and grace, the transient and the transcendent was
closed. Literally, Noyes was a complete enthusiast, completely God filled. On this ground he endeavored to build a
model community, which involved complex marriage,

18. On Finney see, in addition to the works cited immediately
above, his *Memoirs of Rev. Charles G. Finney* (New York: A. S.
Barnes and Company, 1876) and his lectures, *Revivals of Religion*
(Westgate, N.J.: Fleming H. Revell Company, n.d.).

equality of the sexes, systematic mutual criticism, controlled and limited labor, and planned use of leisure time. No other community in the nineteenth century went so far in attempting to educate its members in the delicate areas of interpersonal and intersexual relations. But Noyes, too, faced the problem of sustaining in others, if not in himself, the intensity of experience that he had known in his own conversion and sanctification (or first and second conversions). If one had achieved perfection, where else could he go? It was a view that, augmented by the natural entropy of human life, made for a gradual winding down of the intensity of religious experience in the Oneida Community until that community finally disbanded.[19]

The evangelical Protestant problem of eliciting and sustaining a generative religious experience in early nineteenth-century America is dramatically illustrated in microcosm in the Lyman Beecher family. Lyman, who was born on the eve of the American Revolution and died during the Civil War, became a clinical evangelical leader. Under the tutelage of his Yale mentor Timothy Dwight, followed by more than thirty years in the pastoral ministry, Lyman became an accomplished minister to sick souls. His home was his primary clinic. He sired thirteen children by two wives, and he labored mightily to elicit a conversion experience in every one of the eleven who survived childhood. In the words of his most famous daughter, Harriet Beecher Stowe, who knew full well their meaning,

19. On John Humphrey Noyes see his *Confessions of Religious Experience* (Oneida Reserve: Leonard and Company, 1849), 2–3. Noyes speaks of "a separate education of the heart" and complains that when he was a student at Andover Theological Seminary, "learning was a matter of far greater account with theological students generally, than spirituality." For contemporary accounts of Oneida see Noyes' own writings; Charles Nordhoff, *The Communistic Societies of the United States* (New York: Dover Publications, 1966); and Constance Noyes Robertson, *Oneida Community: An Autobiography, 1851–1876* (Syracuse: Syracuse University Press, 1970).

Lyman pursued every sign of spiritual awakening with "singular and almost indescribable" ardor.[20]

Henry Ward Beecher, his most famous son, labeled Lyman's theological system "*alleviated* Calvinism."[21] The alleviation, however, put even greater pressure on the individual than had unrelieved Calvinism. Lyman lifted the will out of the endless chain of cause and effect into which Calvin and his consistent followers seemed to have bound it. By doing so he gave greater weight to individual effort in the salvation process. At the same time, however, he did not abandon original sin, total depravity, eternal punishment, and the mysterious ways of a righteous but inscrutable deity. The conversion experience was crucial. That determined whether one was bound for heaven or for hell. It was an experience in which one repented for his sin and gave up his own will for God's will. But the experience could not be achieved by will alone. It also required divine action. Still, the individual was under indictment if the experience were not achieved. As Professor Henry F. May correctly points out, Lyman impressed upon his children the conviction that hell was "a real place full of real fire," not a metaphysical abstraction or some sort of mythical concept that could be translated to mean "an absence from God." Without the requisite conversion experience, one would in all probability be "destined to spend an eternity of torture" in this place.[22]

20. The chief published source on the Beecher family is Charles Beecher (ed.), *Autobiography and Correspondence of Lyman Beecher, D.D.* (2 vols.; New York: Harper and Brothers, 1864), which has been reissued under the editorship of Barbara M. Cross (Cambridge: Harvard University Press, 1961). Harriet's statement is from Vol. I, p. 74 of the 1864 edition (and all quotations below are from that edition). According to Harriet, Lyman called his theology "clinical."

21. Quoted in William G. McLoughlin, Jr., *The Meaning of Henry Ward Beecher: An Essay on the Shifting Values of Mid-Victorian America* (New York: Knopf, 1970), 12. Emphasis added.

22. Henry F. May, introduction to Harriet Beecher Stowe, *Old Town Folks* (Cambridge: Harvard University Press, 1966), 8–9. For

Lyman Beecher's views and his personality made for an intense emotional atmosphere in the home and placed a heavy burden on each of the Beecher children. Each reacted in his or her own fashion, and their reactions indicate some of the ways and byways into which the intensity of the Puritan experience led. Without exception among those who left written records (and most of them did), each departed in some way from the father's views. [23] While the father, in his efforts to preserve and advance what he regarded as the essential elements of evangelical Protestant spirituality, stressed sharp discontinuity between God and man and between the old self and the new self, the children came to assert continuity. The father belonged to an elite corps of evangelicals who sought to bring the populace up to the stern demands of a distant

---

Lyman Beecher and his theological views, in particular, see his sermon, "The Faith Once Delivered to the Saints" (selections are included in his autobiography); Stuart C. Henry, *Unvanquished Puritan: A Portrait of Lyman Beecher* (Grand Rapids, Mich.: William B. Eerdman's Publishing Company, 1973); Sidney Earl Mead, *Nathaniel William Taylor, 1786—1858: A Connecticut Liberal* (Hamden, Conn.: Archon Books, 1967); and Vincent Harding, "Lyman Beecher and the Transformation of American Protestantism" (Ph.D. dissertation, University of Chicago, 1965).

23. The most prolific writers among Lyman's offspring were Harriet, Catharine, Henry Ward, Edward, and Charles. In addition, there is Catharine Beecher (ed.), *The Biographical Remains of Rev. George Beecher, 1809—1843* (New York: Leavitt, Trow and Company, 1844). Unpublished Beecher materials abound. Major collections include the Beecher Family Documents, Mount Holyoke College Library, and Papers of the Beecher and Stowe Families, Schlesinger Library, Radcliffe College. I have also consulted the Thomas K. Beecher Papers, Cornell University Library, which include correspondence between Lyman and his youngest son James.

The Beecher family was not only prolific in writing; it was also long-lived. The average length of life of the eleven children who survived infancy was seventy-five years. Two of them were apparently suicides—George, who was cut down at age thirty-four, and James, who lived to his fifty-eighth year. Seven of the eleven who survived to maturity were considered important enough to be included in the *Dictionary of American Biography:* Catharine, Edward, Harriet, Henry Ward, Charles, Isabella Beecher Hooker, and Thomas.

and rigorous ruler God. The children tended to ally themselves increasingly with popular sentiment for a humanized God and a divinized man. In the process, religious experience was either shunted aside in the interest of doing good or trivialized and sentimentalized.

Catharine Beecher, the eldest, after an especially painful period of soul searching as a young woman, chose the way of moral determination. She experienced her most intense spiritual distress upon the occasion of the accidental drowning of her fiancé at a time when the state of his soul was uncertain. So also was the state of Catharine's soul, and for some time after the untimely death of her lover, she agonized about both souls—his and hers. Although she experienced deep sorrow and anguish, she did not and apparently could not have the requisite religious feelings. In a letter to her brother Edward she stated: "I feel no realizing sense of my sinfulness, no love to the Redeemer, nothing but that I am unhappy and need religion; but where or how to find it I know not." Catharine did not have the coveted experience of conversion during this desperate period of her life (or later, so far as the records show). She climbed slowly out of the pit of despair through a resolve "to do good," and she eventually concluded that God had given man the ability so to do. Hence she took refuge in a high-level moralism.[24]

Edward Beecher, Catharine's confidant and the third child in the family, was the first to have the coveted experience. But he also had spiritual problems. He was deeply troubled by the view that made God a wrathful tyrant who punishes man for not doing the good that man

24. For the family correspondence having to do with Catharine's experience following the death of her fiancé, Professor Alexander M. Fisher, see Beecher (ed.), *Autobiography and Correspondence of Lyman Beecher*, I, 478–503, esp. 480, and Edward Beecher to Catharine Beecher, March 29, 1822, in Papers of the Beecher and Stowe Families, Schlesinger Library, Radcliffe College. On Catharine's later views see the following of her writings:

is incapable of doing. This seemed to be his father's view, but it was not congenial to Edward's mind and heart. All through his childhood, according to Catharine's account of what Edward related to her, "as far back as memory could reach he never had a feeling of conscious alienation from God, or of hostility or revolt." At the time of his conversion he sought to know God "face to face, as a man talked with his friend." Seeking such a friend, he turned to the New Testament and found there a God who suffers with man and thus reveals human qualities. Edward was still troubled, however, by the Calvinist notions of original sin, total depravity, and eternal punishment. How could these be squared with the suffering God, the face-to-face friend, that he had found in the New Testament? Finally Edward hit upon the "truth" of the *preexistence of souls*—hardly a Calvinist or Puritan notion! Man in this life atones for sins committed in previous lives, not for the sin of Adam. This "truth" came to him, Edward reported to his younger brother Charles, as "a virtual revelation." But this new view was so unorthodox that he could not summon the courage to publish it abroad until a quarter of a century after the initial revelation in 1827. Old Lyman "had no place in his system for this new revelation" to his son, nor did any of the other "great champions of evangelical faith." But in the intimate circle of his siblings, Edward could privately communicate his views. Charles reports that at the age of fourteen he "instantly as by a kind of intuition" accepted Edward's new doctrine. Sixty years later he wrote that he had "never doubted it since."

Suggestions Respecting Improvements in Education Presented to the Trustees of the Hartford Female Seminary (Hartford: Packard and Butter, 1829); *The Elements of Mental and Moral Philosophy, Founded upon Experience, Reason, and the Bible* (Hartford: n.p., 1831); and *Letters on the Difficulties of Religion* (Hartford: Belknap and Hamersley, 1836). The most recent scholarly biography is Kathryn Kish Sklar, *Catharine Beecher: A Study in American Domesticity* (New Haven: Yale University Press, 1973).

Charles, in fact, carried the doctrine further as he developed a kind of Christian spiritualism.[25]

Edward's "revelation" signaled the beginnings of a profound break with the past. In Edward's view, God was no longer a distant, majestic being who judged man's sin and, through a process known only to Himself, selected some men to be saved and others to be lost. He had become instead a friendly ally in the struggle with the effects of one's former lives. Having thus vindicated God's innocence, the next step was to join the romantics in discovering and vindicating man's innocence. Edward did not take that step. But his view was conducive to blurring the sharpness of distinction between God and man, which was understood by Lyman and his Puritan predecessors to be self-evident.

Edward's revelation was also of keen importance to the spiritual development of his younger sister Harriet, who was perhaps the most complex of the Beecher brood. From early in life Harriet longed for a loving God, and she eagerly turned to the warm, gentle, kindly Jesus and to all evidence of the mother love she had so sorely missed in her own young life. (Her mother Roxanne had died when Harriet was four.) Although something of Lyman's moral and spiritual zeal rubbed off on her, Harriet rejected much of the "alleviated Calvinism" of her father. She chafed under the pressure of the required conversion experience. She joined the Episcopal church out of interest in its stately ceremonialism. And she too flirted with spirit-

25. On Edward's conversion see Beecher (ed.), *Autobiography and Correspondence of Lyman Beecher*, I, 428, 460, 476; Edward Beecher to Catharine Beecher, August, 1822, and Edward to Lyman Beecher, March 27, 1822, in Papers of the Beecher and Stowe Families; and Robert Merideth, *The Politics of the Universe: Edward Beecher, Abolition, and Orthodoxy* (Nashville: Vanderbilt University Press, 1968), 26–27. For an account of Edward's revelation see Merideth, *The Politics of the Universe*, 47–49, and Catharine to Edward, August 23, 1828, in Papers of the Beecher and Stowe Families. For a published version of the views of Charles Beecher see his *Spiritual Manifestations* (Boston: Lee and Shepard, 1879).

ualism. Spiritually, she seems to have moved repeatedly from elation to despair during what she called her "long course of wandering." Constant inner tension and intensity made her early something of a "burned-out case," and late in life she appears to have toyed with experience almost in a fanciful way.[26]

The propensity among the sons and daughters of Lyman Beecher to humanize divinity and divinize human sentiment is most evident in the life and work of Henry Ward Beecher. He early exalted and even worshiped his lost mother Roxanne, who had died when he was little more than a babe in arms. Over a long and influential ministry, which spanned the middle years of the nineteenth century, he also moved farther and farther out of his father's orbit. In the process he came as close as any nineteenth-century minister to being the national chaplain of his time. His sermons were often front-page news. His writings were widely read. He was the object of much adulation. Henry did not speak as clear and distinct a word as Lyman had, however. His published work often seems bland and muddled in comparison with Lyman's. But in that, too, he spoke to his age. It was a time to make the rough edges smooth, to take the harshness out of religion, and to put a smile on the deity's countenance. It was a time to exalt even the humblest sentiment and to give play to even the commonest emotion.[27]

Even though Lyman Beecher's children appropriated

26. On Harriet's spiritual development and problems see Charles E. Stowe (ed.), *The Life of Harriet Beecher Stowe Compiled from Her Letters and Journals* (Boston: Houghton Mifflin Company, 1890), 50; Beecher (ed.), *Autobiography and Correspondence of Lyman Beecher*, II, 487–98; and Charles H. Foster, *The Rungless Ladder: Harriet Beecher Stowe and New England Puritanism* (Durham, N.C.: Duke University Press, 1954).

27. On Henry Ward Beecher see McLoughlin, *The Meaning of Henry Ward Beecher;* Paxton Hibben, *Henry Ward Beecher: An American Portrait* (New York: Press of the Readers Club, 1942); and William C. Beecher and Samuel Scoville, *A Biography of Henry Ward Beecher* (New York: C. L. Webster, 1888).

views that clearly differed from his, most of them still shared his zest for life, his moral zeal, and his Protestant patriotism. There was an enormously human quality about Lyman, and despite all of his advertisements of eternity he thoroughly relished this life. At his last public appearance, when he was well past his allotted threescore and ten, he said that, if God gave him an option either to enter heaven immediately or to begin his life over again and work once more, he *"would enlist again in a minute."*[28] Any true Beecher would have chosen to enlist. That much of the energizing force of Puritanism came through loud and clear. Without that, the second-generation modifications of Lyman's views might simply have thinned out into sheer sentimentalism. But a combination of romantic union and moral zeal was suited to the Beechers and their age.

EXPERIENTIAL SPIRITUALITY
FURTHER GENERALIZED

Preoccupation with intense personal experience also characterized the transcendentalists of antebellum America. Some of them even secretly admired the intensity of the experience of their New England Puritan forebears, and they protested against the spiritual dryness that had come over both New England orthodoxy and Unitarianism. But the transcendentalists transferred the context of religious experience from the realm of grace to the realm of nature, or rather they erased any distinction between the two.

The transcendentalists picked up on that tendency in American religion "to see a spiritual significance in every natural fact," as F. O. Mathiessen put it.[29] But in the

28. Beecher (ed.), *Autobiography and Correspondence of Lyman Beecher*, II, 552.
29. F. O. Mathiessen, *American Renaissance: Art and Expression in the Age of Emerson and Whitman* (New York: Oxford University Press, 1941), 243.

process they both changed the understanding of nature and magnified its role. Nature became both means and end in the achievement of self-validating experience. It was the "transparent eyeball" through which passed life's most vivid and meaningful sensations; it was also the primary arena of self-fulfillment. Hence one must throw himself on the bosom of nature, on the whole wide world with all its "limitless leaves" and "heaped stones." With Emerson, the transcendentalists yielded or sought to yield the individual self to this "perfect whole," to find one's individual soul in the "oversoul."[30]

The way was prepared by this transcendentalist mood for the self to become or to be understood as a series of sensations without prospect of meaning or direction. But that conclusion could be avoided so long as the world and nature in particular were believed to be beneficent. The transcendentalist mood was characterized by this sort of optimism. Transcendentalism was, to use William James's categories, a religious expression of the "healthy-minded" and "once-born" type. James, who himself wanted to be healthy-minded but reluctantly joined the "sick souls," wrote that Emerson had "too little understanding of the morbid side of life."[31]

This healthy-mindedness took popular religious form late in the nineteenth century in the absolute idealism of the New Thought movement, which was to exercise an influence far beyond its institutional expression in such groups as Christian Science. Now the self floated perennially upon a sublime and glassy sea, knowing neither beginning nor end, pain nor death. Now there was not even a need to yield the individual self "to the perfect whole," as Emerson had sought to do by an act of will. The self *was* the

30. See Ralph Waldo Emerson's poem "Each and All" and his essays "Nature" and "Over-Soul."
31. Henry James (ed.), *The Letters of William James* (Boston: Atlantic Monthly Press, 1920), II, 197.

perfect whole or was so much absorbed in it as to be indistinguishable from it. Now there was also no need for an ethic of grace; by a right turn of mind all becomes grace, and everyday life is encased in a protective halo of heavenly light. Beginning with the assumption that "whatever is is good," uncritical idealists could easily jump to the conclusion that "whatever is is right." In its more banal forms, this type of mentality could sanction, with a clear conscience, the most successful forms of money getting and power brokering.[32]

This sort of generalized spirituality may have been one distant product of Puritan experiential spirituality. But, if it was, it completed a movement from stress on an intense, personal, soul concern for that overwhelming influx of supernatural grace, which was a discrete but repeatable experience, to a confident assurance that all of life was absorbed into the godhead itself. Distinctions, discontinuities, ups and downs disappeared, and there was no need for change. Every valley was exalted and every mountain made low. In such an understanding, *all* experience is spiritual and, hence, the notion of experiential spirituality had been radically changed.

THE DIVIDE IN EVANGELICAL PROTESTANTISM

This kind of generalized spirituality also moved out of the orbit of evangelical Protestantism, which had reached its most vigorous maturity early in the nineteenth century and which, as the discussion of the Beechers has intimated, was itself undergoing dramatic change. To foreshorten and simplify a complex story, there occurred at the turn of the twentieth century a significant split in the evangelical Protestant ranks. This split was brought on by differing

32. See Donald Meyer, *The Positive Thinkers: A Study of the American Quest for Health, Wealth, and Personal Power from Mary Baker Eddy to Norman Vincent Peale* (Garden City, N.Y.: Doubleday, 1965).

approaches to the intellectual and socioeconomic revolutions of the late nineteenth century. It involved, among other things, the emergence of two radically different understandings of the nature and role of experiential spirituality.[33]

On the one side there emerged a movement, labeled Fundamentalism, which clung to the earlier evangelical stress on the centrality of the personal conversion experience. But the exigencies of the time appeared to require that that experience be inexorably linked with a stringent biblical literalism, which, when the chips were down, seemed to become even more crucial than the experience itself. The word tended to replace the spirit. Or, to put it another way, to be "authentic" the experience had to be confined within the bounds of a world view that provided a kind of fortress against the onslaughts of modernity. At the same time, this world view tended to ignore the more significant social problems of the day and to bless American enterprise and the prevailing moral system.

On the other side there emerged a movement or a series of movements—called variously the Social Gospel movement, liberal Protestantism, and, more narrowly, Modernism—which rejected biblical literalism and sought directly to relate what was considered to be the prophetic message of the Bible to the social problems of the day. By and large these liberalizing movements tended to turn away from stress on a personal transforming experience. These socially conscious Protestants tended to stress growth, development, evolution, and continuity in the spiritual life and

33. On the division or divisions within Protestantism see Martin E. Marty's discussion of what he calls "the two party system" in *Righteous Empire: The Protestant Experience in America* (New York: Dial Press, 1970), 177; Richard Quebedeaux on the "great Protestant schism" in *The Young Evangelicals* (New York: Harper and Row, 1974), 5–17; and Winthrop S. Hudson on the "new intellectual climate" in *Religion in America* (Rev. ed.; New York: Charles Scribner's Sons, 1973), Chap. 11.

in the historical process. Through proper nurture the individual would reach a point where, under the inspiration of the social vision of the kingdom of God, he would see the need for social change and would help effect it. Collectively, such socially aware Christians would then bring about needed changes in society. These liberalizing tendencies sometimes proved to be more intellectual than spiritual. Here was, perhaps, too bland an approach, neither sufficiently revolutionary in its view of what was required for social change nor sufficiently attentive to intense, personal, generative religious experience.

The split in evangelical Protestantism signaled the significant debilitation and decline of Puritan experiential spirituality in this country. With the truncation or the archaizing of the central element in that religious tradition, much of its vitality was apparently lost. As suggested above, that Puritan Protestant tradition had not been rich in other common elements of religious traditions, such as a cultic system, which might have sustained or even enriched the religious life. Furthermore, although it had once been culture shaping, it had by this time become mostly subordinate to or dependent on other seemingly more dynamic elements in American culture. It is true that, culturally, Protestantism still played an important role in American culture, but that role became increasingly more secondary or even vestigial.

Vigorous efforts were made to revitalize Protestantism in the twentieth century. Perhaps the most significant of these were the so-called neoorthodox and neoevangelical movements. The former, following the lead of such European theologians as Karl Barth and more directly under the dynamic stimulation of the brothers Reinhold and H. Richard Niebuhr in America, reaffirmed the transcendence of God and the sinfulness of man in separation from Him. Here again was a prophetic word. But it was not widely heard. Furthermore, the message lacked experiential reinforcement or undergirding. The neoevangelicals, on the other hand, were loud in calling for the traditional conversion experience but generally quite soft in speaking a prophetic word. By and large they tended to reinforce the link between conservative Protestantism and conservative Americanism.[34]

BEYOND PROTESTANTISM

In the meantime, other religious traditions gained new prominence and perhaps even evidenced new vitality in America. Historians may well regard developments in Roman Catholic circles after mid-century as the most significant religious developments in this period. These include a renewed stress on contemplative practices, a radical social and political critique, and a movement characterized by a renewed sense of the immediacy of the influence of the Holy Spirit. They are significant not only among and for Roman Catholics, but they are also exerting an influence beyond Roman Catholic circles.

It is becoming evident, in fact, that the story of religion in America and especially of experiential spirituality can no longer be told, if it ever could, exclusively or even primarily in terms of the religious traditions. This is well illustrated by Professor Hal Bridges in his treatment of mysticism in twentieth-century America.[35] He includes a Trappist monk, a rabbi, two Quakers, and a black Baptist. (They are Thomas Merton, Abraham Joshua Heschel, Rufus Jones, Thomas Kelly, and Howard Thurman, respectively. He also treats Vedanta and Zen Buddhism.) These men lived during an apparent long, dark night of the soul

34. Ernest R. Sandeen develops the thesis that Fundamentalism is an "authentic conservative tradition" in America in his essay, "Fundamentalism and American Identity," *Annals of the American Academy of Political and Social Science*, No. 387 (January, 1970), 56–65.

35. Hal Bridges, *American Mysticism from William James to Zen* (New York: Harper and Row, 1970).

in America. Yet they experienced and wrote about continued self-transformation through a power greater than
the individual self.

EXPERIENTIAL SPIRITUALITY TODAY

Professor Bridges' book on mysticism was published at a
time (1970) when America was in the midst of a spiritual
upheaval of unprecedented proportions. There was burgeoning evidence of a great, unquenched thirst for validating, integrative, and generative experience. The stress on
experience, which had characterized much of earlier American history, broke out anew, and the experientialists of
that history and of religious history, generally, gained
renewed influence. Pentecostalism flourished as never before in this country. A growing neoevangelical movement,
especially among youth, stressed the "Jesus experience." It
was not clear whether this "Jesus movement" was, by and
large, a replica of earlier evangelical phenomena or something different. One observer called it "that new time
religion"[36] and argued that it could be distinguished from
earlier awakenings in its relative independence of traditional churches and conservative Americanism.

In the meantime, many sought meaningful experience in
what one authority has called the "new religions."[37] Find-
ing Western religious traditions generally lacking in experiential stress, spiritual techniques, and unifying world
views, these people sought to appropriate these apparent
strengths in non-Western religions. Some even hoped to go
to the "mystical core of all religion," and others hoped to
plumb the psychic depths for a perennial substratum called
the "Old Gnosis."[38]

36. Erling Jorstad, *That New Time Religion: The Jesus Revival in
America* (Minneapolis: Augsburg Publishing House, 1972).
37. Jacob Needleman, *The New Religions* (Garden City, N.Y.:
Doubleday, 1970).
38. Theodore Roszak, *Where the Wasteland Ends: Politics and
Transcendence in Postindustrial Society* (Garden City, N.Y.: Doubleday, 1972).

The spiritual revolution of the late sixties also extended well beyond obvious religious channels. Human potentialists, informed by the latest developments in psychology and guided by a humanistic orientation, sought to tap seemingly unreached and unexploited resources within the human animal. This movement was marked by a confidence that people were capable of experiencing new heights of joy and new levels of self-actualization. The movement was quite sophisticated in its efforts to use the insights and techniques afforded by our scientific, technological civilization. Some within it also used the language and techniques of spiritual awareness, quest, and rebirth. Beginning with efforts at self-discovery through others, called encounter, some moved to something akin to mystical contemplation as the primary means of human transformation.[39]

In *Education and Ecstacy*, one of the human potentialists, George B. Leonard, argues that "just to survive . . . we need a new human nature."[40] Expounding a behaviorist mysticism, Leonard finds sources of this newness in the vast, mostly untapped resources of the human brain and in the world around us. He argues for an educational content radically altered from that which characterized our "civilized epoch." Educational style must also be extraordinary, as Leonard suggests in a chapter entitled "The Rogue as Teacher." One of the most advanced types of "rogue," says Leonard, is the mystic. The mystic *sees* in an extraordinary fashion. He experiences reality as it is, not as it seems or as society packages it; he is in touch with the deep-seated potential within himself and in his world. And he knows ecstasy, "the ultimate experience."

It may seem strange that in our highly advanced and

---

39. On the spiritual aspects of the human-potential movement, see, for a sampling, the works of Sam Keen, George B. Leonard, and Abraham Maslow.

40. George B. Leonard, *Education and Ecstasy* (New York: Dell Publishing Company, 1968), 7, 96, Chap. 13.

powerful technological society we hear again of the quest
for "the ultimate experience." Apparently no amount of
electronic gadgeteering can provide complete escape from
that curious human predicament that only in transport or
transformation is the self really quickened. That is worth
noting even though much of the current quest for ecstacy
appears to be primarily a desire to *feel* intensely. Some
have apparently been pushed to the point where they must
feel in order to know that they are alive.

At this point it may be helpful to remind ourselves that,
in the words of Henri Bergson, "the soul of the great
mystic does not stop at ecstacy, as at the end of a journey." Mystical ecstacy may seem to be repose, but it is a
repose like that of a locomotive standing in a station under
a head of steam. Such a person has the capacity to
help effect a change in humanity.[41] Bergson here brings
together the two requisite elements in his "dynamic religion"—decisive, transforming personal experience and creative social act.

Bergson speaks, however, of the *great* mystic and
thereby seems to imply that this kind of experience is
open only to a few select spiritual virtuosos. But there is
also validity in that traditional Puritan Protestant stress on
an experience possible even for the most humble man or
woman and in the most humble of circumstances. While it
is true that the Puritans affirmed a theological view of
election or selectivity, if they followed their theology to a
logical conclusion they had also finally to affirm that
people could do nothing about their own election. Hence,
logically, the Puritan view held out the real possibility of
surprise, the possibility that anyone under almost any
circumstances might be enabled to drink the elixir of
God's transforming grace, might experience—to use a favorite figure of Jonathan Edwards—something akin to the

41. Bergson, *The Two Sources of Morality and Religion*, 219.

indescribable delicacy and delight of the taste of honey. That figure suggests immediacy and earthiness. It suggests that experience of the transforming grace of God does not require an extraordinary act of the will or heroic separation from the affairs of this world; that experience may come, in fact, in connection with very ordinary employments.

Puritan experiential spirituality is a significant factor in the American heritage. Furthermore, the fusion in the Puritan experience of dynamic transcendence with experiential religion had a powerful potential for both openness and commitment in a person's approach to his own life and to others. That potential may still exist today, but the Puritan contextual concepts probably need to be translated into a modern idiom if that potential is to be significantly real in our time. Post-Puritan generations, our own included, have had both intellectual and moral difficulties with the Puritan understanding of God. It is not my intention to defend that concept or to offer a systematic restatement of it for the present age. Suffice it to say that the underlying truth in the Puritan understanding of man in relation to God apparently remains as true today as it was in the seventeenth century or as it was for Saint Augustine over one thousand years earlier. Our souls are restless until they find rest in God—that is, we are aspiring, incomplete, and unfulfilled creatures who seek a companionship that rises above the mundane affairs of this world. What the Puritans did with that truth is the main point of this chapter: They found that companionship in the mundane affairs of this world. They affirmed and knew the reality of transformation in and of daily experience. No doubt they "often confused the trifling with the important," as Robert Ulich puts it.[42] But what counts most in the final analysis is that they "knew of the great

42. Ulich, *A History of Religious Education*, 157.

and transcendent" in their daily lives, and this makes the decisive difference between them and many who came after them.

To put together the great and the transcendent with the ordinary is no small task; in fact, one may understand it as a gift, as the Puritans understood it to be. Some unusually sensitive folk may begin with the power of mystical vision and move to this world. Others may only begin with ordinary experience. But that may be a significant beginning if one can know and reflect on both the limits and the openness in that experience. Ordinary experience does confront us with limits—we are who we are in this particular time and place, under these particular circumstances. Such experience can be conducive to despair and a sense of meaninglessness. But ordinary experience may also be illumined by a sense of openness, transformed by a sense of power, heightened by a sense of meaning. Finally, both limit and openness may be embraced in the faith that, to put it in traditional language, "whether we live or whether we die, we are the Lord's"[43] or, to put it in a more modern form, "everything . . . has a meaning." That is not to say that everything is either perfectly plain or fully coherent, in some new gnostic fashion, but that "there is nothing intrinsically meaningless." With this experience-oriented faith, which still may seem like a gift, "every act of consciousness is an act of discovery and every deed an act of creativity."[44]

43. Romans 14:8, Revised Standard Version.

44. Richard R. Niebuhr, *Experiential Religion* (New York: Harper and Row, 1972), 43. Niebuhr uses a quotation from Dag Hammarskjöld's *Markings* as a basis for the development of this view. *Experiential Religion* is a recent creative effort to restate, in contemporary language, the basic thrust of the Puritan stress on experiential spirituality.

4

Seeking Soul
in a Civil Society

"Justice is the end of civil society."—James Madison

Civil—"public or social order"; "naturally good or virtuous but
unregenerate," hence *"civil righteousness."*
—*Oxford English Dictionary*

The position of Roger Williams "is a plea for an awareness of the
infinite depths of human consciousness."—Perry Miller

We have examined the American search for soul as expressed in (1) the confident sense of a unique new beginning in this world, (2) the quest for a distinctively American identity, and (3) the more clearly religious view and
experience of soul rebirth. We turn in this chapter to one
more significant aspect of the American context that has
helped to nurture or at least to make possible the search
for soul—*i.e.*, the idea of a civil society. The essence of that
idea, which was developed in America, among other places,
in the seventeenth and eighteenth centuries, is that the
primary end or purpose of a civil society is a limited or
this-worldly one, such as just and orderly relations among
people. The other side of that coin is the conviction that
the state is not competent to provide ultimate salvation for
the human soul.

The idea of a civil society is clearly formalized in the
American Constitution. The Preamble speaks of establish-
ing justice and insuring domestic tranquillity as being
among the primary goals of "we the people of the United
States." The First Amendment begins with the words
"Congress shall make no law respecting an establishment

83

of religion, or prohibiting the free exercise thereof." These provisions relative to religion, which represented a profound departure from the past, were thought by many citizens of the new nation to be crucial to the realization of a civil society.

In a sense the American venture is an experiment that tests whether it is possible for the people, once having ordained and established their civil polity in the Constitution, subsequently to live by it. Or, to put it more broadly, this is an experiment that tests whether a civil society is possible. The results of the experiment are variously judged, but one thing is clear: A functioning civil society is conditional on the attainment of a relatively high degree of moral and spiritual integrity among the citizens. The achievement of justice, for example, depends generally on a citizenry in which the sense of justice is developed, exercised, and renewed rather than left to atrophy and, more specifically, on the selection and election of men and women who seek faithfully to make, execute, and uphold the laws designed to realize justice. And the carrying out of the provisions of the Constitution that have to do with religion depends on the realization among the populace of a condition of spiritual strength that precludes the necessity to rely on the state for spiritual fulfillment.

What follows is a reflective analysis of selected, significant aspects of the genesis and development of this American civil experiment, not a systematic treatment. Roger Williams is selected from the colonists because he is one of the most interesting American experimenters and was perhaps the most profound and revolutionary in his time. He combined experiential spirituality and the search for a civil society in a way that was not only of considerable historical significance but is also still instructive. The significance of our next subject, the American Founding Fathers' embodiment of the idea of a civil society in the civil polity that they called the Constitution of the United States, is self-evident. The welfare of our civil society depends to a considerable extent on a continued dialogue with them. Finally, we consider more directly those elements of moral and spiritual integrity on which that civil society depends.

ROGER WILLIAMS: SEEKER AND CITIZEN

Roger Williams demonstrated, near the dawn of American history, that ideological uniformity is neither necessary nor conducive to maximum human development, that vital spirituality may involve continuing search, and that a relatively peaceful society could be achieved in a civil as against a religious state if men would practice what was called "civil righteousness"—that is, judicious self-restraint and responsible public commitment as citizens. Williams was, as noted above, very much a Puritan on such matters as biblical authority and experiential spirituality. But he differed sharply from most of his fellow Puritans on the personal and communal implications of biblical religion and "experimental divinity." Most of his adult life he was spiritually, by his own profession, a "seeker." And most of that time he was the most influential political figure in a "civil state" described by one of his associates as "a lively experiment ... with full liberty in religious concernments."[1]

While the Puritans stressed the centrality of the experience of saving faith and while individually they agonized much over that experience—now being assured, now lacking assurance—they had few such doubts about the divine validity of their collective endeavors in church and state. On the contrary, they understood themselves to be establishing a biblical commonwealth or *the* biblical commonwealth; they thought that their church and state were

1. John Clarke, "Second Address from Rhode Island to King Charles the Second," in John Russell Bartlett (ed.), *Records of the Colony of Rhode Island and Providence Plantations in New England* (Providence: A. C. Green and Brothers, 1856), I, 490–91.

earthly embodiments of God's eternal truth as revealed in
the Bible. They were, in their own imaginings, like a city
upon a hill, an example, a model for all the world to see.
But their model was a closed community. One conformed
or got out. As one of their number, Nathaniel Ward, put it,
the only liberty allowed to those who did not agree with
these Puritans in religious and political matters was the
"free liberty to keep away from us."[2] The potential dynamism in their experiential spirituality, a potential openness
rooted in a concept of dynamic deity and in the fact that
words and institutional forms can never fully contain or
encompass experience, was lost or ignored in their approach to church and state. These children of protestors
against the infallible Roman Catholic church and pontiff
merely substituted their own infallible institutions and
selves for those of Rome.

Seeker

It took a Williams to appropriate the dynamism in Puritan experiential spirituality and to carry it to logical con-
clusions. Williams, who is sometimes understood or misun-
derstood as a seventeenth-century Thomas Jefferson, was,
if anything, even more religious than most of his fellow
Puritans. And the logic of his religion led him to espouse,
primarily for spiritual and not political reasons, liberty of
conscience and separation of church from state and from
the world generally and to launch an experiment in civil
politics. Williams employed the metaphor of the "wall of
separation" between church and state long before Thomas
Jefferson did, but Williams used it to stress the religious
life and the purity of the church rather than to preserve
the independence of the state. In the name of that "soul
liberty" instituted by Christ, who freed men spiritually

2. Quoted in Perry Miller (ed.), *The American Puritans: Their
Poetry and Prose* (Garden City, N.Y.: Doubleday and Company,
1956), 97.

from all earthly kingdoms, Williams denied that civil authorities had any right to tamper with religious matters.[3]

Williams was also unwilling to accept any living ecclesiastical figure as final authority over his soul. He concluded, as Perry Miller has put it, that no man or group of men here and now could say for certain or completely embody "what is ultimate truth."[4] He did not deny ultimate truth; he only affirmed that God, the discloser of ultimate truth or the embodiment of that truth, had not yet completed His purposes with man. In the meantime, one had no alternative but to wait and to seek—that is, to search the Scriptures, the signs of the time, and one's own experience for evidence of the final consummation of God's redeeming work. And, after brief affiliations with various religious groups or churches, Williams finally abandoned all hope of locating the true church of God in his lifetime and gave himself up to being a seeker in matters of the spirit.[5]

The arrogance of those imperial Christians who thought they had the keys to the kingdom of God in their own hands much offended Williams. These men who neatly bottled Christ inordinately constricted human spirituality. He reminded them that God had revealed Himself fully in a man "who past through this World with the esteeme of a

3. Williams wrote of a hedge or "wall of separation" between the "garden of the church and the wilderness of the world" in Roger Williams, *Complete Writings of Roger Williams* (New York: Russell and Russell, 1963), I, 392. See also Perry Miller, *Roger Williams: His Contributions to the American Tradition* (New York: Atheneum, 1965), 89, 98. On similarities and differences between Williams and Jefferson see Mark DeWolfe Howe, *The Garden and the Wilderness: Religion and Government in American Constitutional History* (Chicago: University of Chicago Press, 1965).

4. Perry Miller, introduction to Williams, *Complete Writings*, VII, 23.

5. For Williams on the true church see the *Complete Writings*, I, 36, 361, and his treatise on "The Hireling Ministry None of Christs," *Complete Writings*, VII, 142–91. See also Miller, *Roger Williams*, 96, 198–99, 253, and Winthrop S. Hudson (ed.), *Experiments of Spiritual Life and Health by Roger Williams* (Philadelphia: Westminster Press, 1951), 16–17.

Mad man, a Deceiver, a Conjurer, a Traytor against Caesar,
and . . . at last chose to depart on the stage of a pianfull
shamefull Gibbet. . . . If thou seekest in these searching
times," he concluded, "mak'st him alone thy . . . soules
beloved, willing to follow and be like him in doing, in
suffring," even though his "first Patterne" may not have
been fully restored. It is not without reason that the late
Perry Miller concluded one of the last things he wrote on
Roger Williams with the words: "To learn to know, even a
little, the mind and heart of Roger Williams . . . is to find
the world ecstatically and generously turned upside
down."[6]

Professor Miller also wrote in that same context that
Williams' position "is a plea for an awareness of the infinite depths of human consciousness."[7] This is to describe
Williams in modern language, but it is to draw a warranted
conclusion. True, Williams was nurtured in the Puritan
environment of early seventeenth-century England, and he
was orthodox in most of his theological positions. But just
as he moved physically from the centers of orthodox
Puritan power in England and Massachusetts Bay to the
extreme outer edges of that power in the Rhode Island
wilderness, where he could practice "soul liberty," so,
under the conviction of ultimate certainties not yet revealed, he moved mentally and spiritually away from the
proximate certainties of Puritan orthodoxy to the outer
edges of that orthodoxy, where he could fully practice the
"liberty of seeking."

This is not to argue that Williams was either a skeptic or
an agnostic. He was convinced of the rightness of his own
analysis of the truth as disclosed in the Bible. But that
analysis led him to conclude that God had still more truth
to disclose. Hence one should continue to seek. Nor is it to

6. Williams, *Complete Writings*, I, 317–18, and Miller in Williams, *Complete Writings*, VII, 25.
7. *Ibid.*, VII, 24.

contend that Williams was blandly tolerant of those who disagreed with him on questions of biblical interpretation. In fact he could be very sharp in controversy on such questions, as he was with some Quakers, for example. But he did not take up arms against his opponents. On the contrary, he endeavored to live in civil order even with those who differed markedly from him in their theological views.

Citizen

Early in his life Williams urged his friend John Winthrop to "abstract yourselfe with a holy violence from the Dung heape of the Earth."[8] And Williams seems to have been, in those early years, something of a frantic pilgrim himself as he sought to catapult himself off the "Dung heape." But, unlike some other seekers, he did not continue to carry his otherworldliness to either ascetic or political extremes, and he was not so otherworldly as to neglect the demands of this life. On the contrary, during the last forty-five years of his life he devoted extraordinary energies to the affairs of this world—as a family man, a trader, a lay physician, a friend of whites and Indians alike, and, above all, a dedicated citizen and capable leader in various political endeavors.

Williams was extraordinary in many ways. He developed, for example, an unusually close relationship with the native Americans, a relationship that belies the popular picture of the narrowly arrogant Christian who sought, by force if necessary, to convert or to exterminate the "savages." Savages they were, in Williams' understanding. But that meant only that he understood the American Indians to be uncivilized in the sense that they did not possess a literature or practice complex forms of commerce. But in the eyes of God, according to Williams' outlook, they were

8. *Ibid.*, VI, 11.

not necessarily inferior to the seemingly most civilized, professing Christians. Hence Williams endeavored always to treat the Indians as fellow human beings. He learned the languages of the nearest tribes so that he could communicate with them. He defended their property rights. He refused to missionize them unless they asked him to do so. And he endeavored throughout a long lifetime in Rhode Island to secure and advance relatively amicable relations between them and the whites.[9]

Williams was, then, a profoundly otherworldly worldling. While tending his own soul he also looked to the welfare of others. (Governor Edward Winslow of Plymouth Colony called Williams "the sweetest soul I ever knew.")[10] He served the colony of Rhode Island in many ways—as intermediary with the mother country as well as with the Indians, as a counselor, and as governor. When he was well over seventy years old he took part as a soldier and a negotiator in the major Indian campaign of the seventeenth century, King Philip's War. He died impoverished and was buried with military honors.

Williams is most remembered for his contribution to the achievement of religious liberty. He rightly deserves a place of honor as one of the earliest men in Christendom to rebel successfully against the pattern and principle of reli-

9. Williams had a keen sense of the difficulties involved in attempting to communicate with the Indians on spiritual matters. For his time he had a quite sophisticated awareness of the depth of cultural influence and hence difference. Indeed, he not only surpassed most of his contemporaries in that regard, but also many American religious leaders who came after him. "In matters of Earth," he wrote in *Complete Writings*, VII, 40, "men will helpe to spell each other out, but in matters of Heaven . . . how far are the Eares of man hedged up from listening to all improper Language?" This statement was made in his treatise, "Christenings make not Christians, or a Briefe Discourse concerning the name *Heathen*, commonly given to the Indians; as also concerning that great point of their conversion." See also his "A Key into the Language of America," *Complete Writings*, I, 61—285.

10. Quoted by Perry Miller in Williams, *Complete Writings*, VII, 15.

gious uniformity and to lead in setting up an independent
or semiindependent state, whose laws and principles of
order differed categorically from those of other states in
providing religious liberty. It was a truly civil state in that
it was not allied with a particular religion, it did not
pretend to the realization of religious ends, and it was
founded on a common civil agreement and commitment
by its citizens. Williams "knew," writes Cushing Strout,
"that political competence and sainthood were not caus-
ally linked, that human society had its own forms of
civility that made peace and heresy compatible."[11]

Civil Righteousness

Williams was not primarily a political theorist, and he did
not develop a systematic statement of a civil polity. But, in
his debate with John Cotton over what Williams called
"the bloudy tennent of persecution for cause of conscience," he did go some distance toward stating a rationale for a civil state. In that debate Williams defined the
civil state as one that rises from the people's choice and
whose object is "the common-weal, or safety of [the]
people in their bodies and goods." He also maintained that
the principles undergirding what he called "civil magistry"
were universal. "Civil Government is an Ordinance of
God," Williams asserted—that is, God, in his wisdom, has
provided sufficient grace through natural laws or principles
for people, whether saints or not, to govern themselves in
this world and for this-worldly ends. But God does not
require for civil order the following of a specific religion.
Nor does He regard such a civil state as being in any special
sense his kingdom or the fulfillment of his ultimate purpose. Hence, Williams argued, Cotton was wrong in his
conviction that the church in New England was built
according to God's blueprint and therefore had, by divine

11. Cushing Strout, *The New Heavens and New Earth: Political
Religion in America* (New York: Harper and Row, 1974), 22.

right, power to persecute through the state the presumed unbelievers or false believers. He was also wrong in assuming that there was *anything* divinely unique about the Puritan political endeavor in New England or about New England generally.[12]

In his understanding of civility and civil politics Williams seems to have agreed with certain English, Puritan moral and political theologians, including his friend John Milton. *Civil* was understood then, as now, to refer to citizen, citizenship, and the body politic, on the one hand, or as being synonymous with well mannered, orderly, and polite (hence, *civility*), on the other. But some seventeenth-century English thinkers also used it on occasion to mean naturally good or virtuous without being divinely regenerated, moral but not religious. In this sense one could speak of a "civil righteousness," which is grounded in a naturally endowed or God-given potential for virtue, developed through what one Puritan theologian, William Sclater, called "meere morall education" and evidenced in controlled public action. This notion of civil righteousness was primarily a moral, not a religious, notion. It was distinguished from spiritual, saving, or godly righteousness; while it might be essential to common this-worldly relations, it clearly fell short of ultimate salvation. The natural, unredeemed man, the man who had not felt the power of God "to change and renew," could be taught, as Sclater pointed out, to follow "the Law of Nature," to be "careful of common honestie in matters of contract and traffique with men," to live "in obedience to Civill Lawes," and to know and seek to carry out the "duties of the second Table" (commandments five through ten of the Ten Commandments).[13]

12. Williams, *Complete Writings*, III, 354, 249, I, 359–61. See also Richard Reinitz, *Tensions in American Puritanism* (New York: Wiley, 1970), 157–58.
13. William Sclater, *Exposition of I Thessalonians* (London: n.p., 1630), 40–44. See also John Milton, "The Reasons of Church-Gov-

This point of view quite logically led to the conclusion that, although citizenship required civil righteousness, it did not require saving righteousness. Hence rule by the saints was not essential to civil order. Some of the seventeenth-century English moral and political theologians, in part as a result of their experience in the Puritan Commonwealth, reached that conclusion. It was also clearly advanced by Roger Williams and more fully developed subsequently by John Locke.

Establishing a Civil State in Rhode Island

Williams attempted to carry out civil principles initially in the founding of Providence and subsequently in the forming of the colony of Rhode Island. The original agreement entered into by the settlers of Providence was a simple compact under which they agreed to abide by the will of the majority of voters (heads of families) "only in civil things." In 1640 a model for the peace and government of the town was drawn up and signed by thirty-nine inhabitants. The signatories agreed, among other things, "to hould forth liberty of Conscience." They endeavored to establish a system of government on the basis of what they understood to be "common humanity betweene man and man." And the bulk of the document deals with providing a system of "government by way of arbitration" for handling those instances in which that "common humanity" might be refused by "unreasonable persons." Subsequent official or formal agreements in the Rhode Island area repeatedly affirm religious liberty while attempting to work out the details of civil government.[14]

Domestic peace and tranquillity proved to be elusive

---

ernment urg'd against Prelacy," *The Works of John Milton* (New York: Columbia University Press, 1931), Vol. III, Pt. 2.

14. Bartlett (ed.), *Records of the Colony of Rhode Island*, I, 14, 27–31, 113. The Newport agreement of 1641 indicated "that none bee accounted a Delinquent for *Doctrine:* Provided it be not directly repugnant to ye Government or Lawes established."

among the diverse strong- and weak-minded men and
women who were attracted to the relative freedom permitted by the varied civil experiments in the Naragansett
Bay area. Some, "on grounds of conscience" or by claim to
divine direction, seemed to prefer no government at all.
Amid the various political crises and controversies that
marked the early history of the area, Williams tried to steer
a middle course between the Scylla of religious uniformity,
which was after all a means of maintaining order, and the
Charybdis of religious libertarianism, which proclaimed in
effect that, in the name of a presumed "infinite liberty of
conscience," any man could do as he pleased. Williams
consistently maintained that the "lively experiment" in
civil affairs required an adherence to agreed-upon controls
and the achievement of civil righteousness among its citizens. As Edmund S. Morgan has pointed out, Williams
believed that "human beings could live together . . . in
'civility' only by honoring the commands which their
creator had given them."[15] Hence, although Williams was
a religious libertarian, he was not a moral libertarian. He
saw no way that civil society could function without a
degree of moral rectitude among citizens. In both these
views as well as in his efforts to establish a civil state, he
anticipated the eighteenth-century American Founding
Fathers.

THE AMERICAN CIVIL POLITY

The framers of the American Constitution, who seem to
have been little influenced directly by Williams, did legal-
ize his chief concern: the separation of church and state
and the guarantee of religious liberty. They also endeav-

15. Edmund S. Morgan, *Roger Williams, the Church, and the State*
(New York: Harcourt, Brace and World, 1967), 128. On Williams'
attempt to establish a civil society and the difficulties encountered,
see Hudson (ed.), *Experiments of Spiritual Life and Health*, 16; and
Williams, *Complete Writings*, I, 38, 41, VI, 278–79.

ored to establish a civil rather than a religious state, and, to that end, they developed a far more systematic civil polity than Williams had. They too assumed that moral rectitude was essential to the functioning of a civil society, and they supported or cultivated what they regarded as the means— chiefly educational, secondarily religious—for the development of civil righteousness. In these various efforts they showed the influence of both that sober kind of Protestant outlook advanced by Williams and the somewhat more confident outlook of the Enlightenment.

The Founding Fathers assumed that people have a capacity for self-government. Man is a potentially reasonable animal; he is not guided solely by blind instinct or selfish whim. Hence he can rationally seek to govern himself and to agree with his neighbors in the formation of a civil government. They also affirmed the *right* to self-government, and they grounded that right in "Nature and Nature's God." As G. K. Chesterton once put it, "America . . . is founded on a creed." That creed, although rooted in an ultimate ground, is essentially civil in its content and its political implications. It involves, as Chesterton put it, "the pure classical conception that no man must aspire to be anything more than a citizen, and that no man shall endure to be anything less."[16] By implication the creedal affirmation suggested that a civil society is no respecter of persons, that it sanctions neither special privilege nor categorical denial of rights. (Practice, of course, has been quite something else.)

Rights, even "unalienable rights," must be secured. A creedal affirmation requires self-conscious commitment in deed as well as word. The Founding Fathers understood themselves to be agreeing to a civil covenant to secure their rights. It was a covenanted people who declared their

16. G. K. Chesterton, *What I Saw in America* (New York: Dodd, Mead and Company, 1922), 7, 16.

independence and launched the new nation ("we the people"). To this day that covenantal process continues in a formal way when representatives of the people swear or affirm their intention to uphold and defend the fundamental document on which this nation was constituted.

The Founding Fathers worked out the political implications of their views of man and society in the civil polity embodied in the Constitution and the Bill of Rights. That polity is man centered, and it is both minimalistic and open ended. It roots government in the consent of citizens; it protects individuals against infringement by government and other institutions; and it affirms the right of dissent. Indeed, this polity exalts freedom of expression and enables or even encourages differences of view and style within the limits of the common good. At the same time, while it is conducive to the creation of a functioning civil government and to the free development of individuals and groups, large areas of human behavior and aspiration are affected or implicated only indirectly. The framers of the Declaration of Independence affirmed an inalienable human right to pursue human happiness; the framers of the Constitution did not understand themselves to be providing a governmental structure that would guarantee the achievement of that happiness either here or hereafter. The end of civil government, said James Madison, is justice. [17] It is not human happiness or glorifying God and enjoying him forever, even though a civil government makes such pursuits freely possible.

The civil polity is minimalistic and realistic in providing hedges against the vagaries of human nature and hence against the threat of the tyranny of one citizen or group over another. If men were angels, wrote Madison in one of the *Federalist Papers* in defense of the Constitution, there

17. Benjamin Fletcher Wright (ed.), *The Federalist by Alexander Hamilton, James Madison, and John Jay* (Cambridge: Harvard University Press, 1961), 358.

would be no need for government. Even if only the governors were angels, there would be no need for measures to restrict them. But the problem was to constitute a system that would enable men to govern men *and* assure that the governors would also be governed.[18] This required some degree of restraint upon men by law (a government of laws, not men, as it is popularly expressed) and by a governmental system of checks and balances.

Finally, the civil polity eschews any notion of the divine right of a particular individual or group to rule, of an established church, of a theological confession of any sort, and of any required religious practice. As embodied in the Constitution and the Bill of Rights, the polity does not provide for a civil religion. In fact, the First Amendment specifically precludes "an establishment of religion" (note: not *a* religion but *religion* without the article). Government was understood by the Founding Fathers to be a human and necessary convenience but not a sacred institution. The Declaration of Independence grounded human rights and human equality in "Nature and Nature's God," but the later and more authoritative documents do not even appeal to that ground. In fact, there is no reference to the deity at all in those documents.

Of course the Founding Fathers assumed many things that were not actually embodied in the civil polity formalized in the Constitution and the Bill of Rights. Even though the name of God is not mentioned in those documents, they obviously believed in God. And they drew various implications from that belief, some of which have been discussed in chapter one and some of which we shall examine more fully below. They also believed in a common morality and in the necessity for civil righteousness in the successful embodiment of the civil polity. And, believing in immortality, they perhaps assumed that God would

18. *Ibid.*, 356.

ultimately reward civil righteousness as He was sure to
reward generally good moral behavior. In the meantime,
however, as President John F. Kennedy was to put it much
later, "here on earth God's work must truly be our
own."[19] That suggests that government is a human enterprise depending for its success upon the wisdom, efforts,
and civil righteousness of men. It might even also suggest
that this righteousness has to be cultivated, that men of
virtue are not born that way but have to be "raised up."
The Founding Fathers firmly believed both. Government
would not work unless worked at, and the long-range
welfare of the nation depended on the education of an
informed and civilly virtuous citizenry. The one most
notable area in which Jefferson, a convinced, small *r* republican, clearly supported an extension of governmental
activity was formal education. Like William Sclater, Jefferson believed that through moral education people could be
taught to follow "the Law of Nature" and to practice
"common honestie in matters of contract and traffique
with men."[20] And he was convinced that such education
was essential to the well-being of the Republic. Hence he
labored hard to effect a universal system of public education whose ends were civil, not religious, in nature.[21]

The search for the soul of America must not overlook
this civil foundation: the classical conception of citizenship, the human and limited ends of government, and the
assumption of the indispensability to government of civil

19. Davis Newton Lott (ed.), *The Presidents Speak: Inaugural
Addresses of the American Presidents from Washington to Nixon*
(3rd ed.; New York: Holt, Rinehart and Winston, 1969), 271.
20. Sclater, *Exposition of I Thessalonians,* 40–44.
21. For Jefferson on education see Michaelsen, *Piety in the Public
School: Trends and Issues in the Relationship Between Religion and
the Public School in the United States* (New York: Macmillan
Company, 1970), 79–85; Robert M. Healey, *Jefferson on Religion in
Public Education* (New Haven: Yale University Press, 1962); and
Charles Flinn Arrowood (ed.), *Thomas Jefferson and Education in a
Republic* (New York: McGraw-Hill Book Company, 1930).

righteousness. An understanding of that soul in terms of ultimate uniqueness or divinely sanctioned exceptionality runs counter to that essential civility. It is true that the Founding Fathers grounded that civility in an ultimate authority beyond the civil society, "Nature and Nature's God." But their belief in God could and did have a double effect. On the one hand, it served as the ultimate deterrent to any human claim to uniqueness or special privilege, thus essentially as a reinforcement of civility. One of Jefferson's favorite mottoes, Rebellion to Tyrants Is Obedience to God,[22] could be understood as expressive of such a point of view so long as the rebellion did not itself become a new form of tyranny. Perhaps an even more classic expression of this point of view was uttered by Lincoln in his second inaugural address: "The Almighty has His own purposes." In context, Lincoln implied that people, even Americans or citizens of the Union, did not, and perhaps even could not, fully know those purposes.

On the other hand, belief in God could and sometimes did have the very opposite effect: the assertion of American chosenness and sanctification. The Puritan sense of exceptionalism (the city on the hill) and the enthusiastic universalism of the Enlightenment combined to produce in the nineteenth century a common conviction of the moral superiority and universal mission of this "redeemer nation."[23] Such a conviction departed from the civil foundation and also threatened the very "soul liberty" that this foundation sought to protect and encourage.

The American Founding Fathers at times affirmed both positions—*i.e.*, God as the ultimate hedge against national idolatry and God as the sanctifier of the *novus ordo seclorum*. Still, in formalizing both religious liberty and a

22. This was the motto on Jefferson's seal. See Sarah N. Randolph, *The Domestic Life of Thomas Jefferson* (New York: Harper and Brothers, 1871), title page.
23. Ernest Lee Tuveson, *Redeemer Nation: The Idea of America's Millennial Role* (Chicago: University of Chicago Press, 1968).

provision against a congressional establishment of religion,
they built into their civil polity certain hedges against state
worship. Furthermore, as I have suggested, they were
rather restrained and cautious with regard to civil religion.
This caution becomes clearly evident when they are compared with their counterparts in the French Revolution.
The French were more optimistic about unencumbered
human nature's capacity for goodness and more given to
romantic enthusiasms. They assumed that, by throwing off
the tyrannies of the old order and instituting the rights of
man in the new republic, they would almost automatically
bring human virtue and innocence to the fore. Although
there were similarities between the ideologies of the two
groups of revolutionaries, the Americans' view of the ultimate grounding of that ideology tended to be more abstract, more pristine, and less susceptible to human ap-
propriation than was that of the French. The French
revolutionaries attempted at various times directly to establish or put into practice various forms of civil religion,
including the worship of the Supreme Being, the worship
of Nature, and the worship of Man.[24] The Americans did
not make similar efforts. It is true that there were attempts
in the late eighteenth century to effect a "republican
religion," but these efforts, which were short-lived and
unsuccessful, were supported by few of the Founding
Fathers.[25] In the final analysis, religious development was

24. On religion and the French Revolution see François Victor
Alphonse Aulard, *Christianity and the French Revolution*, trans.
Lady Frazer (New York: H. Fertig, 1966), and Christopher Dawson,
The Gods of Revolution (New York: University Press, 1972).

25. On religion and the American Revolution see Edward Frank
Humphrey, *Nationalism and Religion in America, 1774–1789* (Bos-
ton: Chipman Law Publishing Company, 1924); Koch, *Republican
Religion: The American Revolution and the Cult of Reason* (New
York: Henry Holt and Company, 1933); and Perry Miller, "From
the Covenant to the Revival," in James Ward Smith and A. Leland
Jamison (eds.), *The Shaping of American Religion* (Princeton:
Princeton University Press, 1961), 322–68.

up to the individual and to groups of individuals, not to the state or nation. What the state required for its functioning was civil righteousness in citizens, not a particular kind of religious belief and practice, and dedicated civic commitment, not ultimate loyalty.

TOWARD A CIVIL SOCIETY

Civil politics have not been easily achieved in America. This nation, understood as the *novus ordo seclorum*, has been looked to by hopeful, aspiring citizens, both converts and birthright Americans, to provide more even than justice—as if that goal in itself were not task enough. More fortunate Americans, those who have "arrived" or "made it," have looked to the state to protect their gains. Committed to a monolithic Americanism, drawn in their own image, they have seen any threat to that Americanism as a threat to their own salvation.

By their very nature civil politics face difficulties. They "do not stir the passions," as Professor Edward A. Shils points out.[26] But it seems to be a common human tendency to want an ultimate sanction for one's politics. Whether or not that is the case, it is clear that, in recent times especially, the political realm has increasingly assumed a kind of religious role and nation-states have become sole or primary instruments of salvation. In the all-too-realistic brave new worlds imagined by novelists, the state controls the passions, perhaps permitting some degree of individual indulgence, but only on condition of complete loyalty.[27] The tendency to make politics religious or absolute has been further exacerbated in our time by a rapidly developing technology. As D. W. Brogan points out, "a technically unified society may be the

26. Edward A. Shils, *The Intellectuals and the Powers and Other Essays* (Chicago: University of Chicago Press, 1972), 60.
27. For example, Aldous Huxley, *Brave New World*, George Orwell, *1984*, and Kurt Vonnegut, Jr., *Utopia 14*.

enemy, not the friend, of the idea of citizenship."[28] Such a society tends to reduce the potential for rational individual participation in the processes of civil government. The choices that count are generally made by a bureaucracy, which is prone to require unquestioning loyalty of citizens.

Furthermore, the very notion of civility or civil politics is under fire these days. It has never been uncommon, of course, for skeptics to deny that human beings have the ability to join in civil concert with others for the achievement of limited ends. In the eyes of such skeptics people must be governed; they cannot govern themselves. But civil politics are more attacked today by those who wish for and espouse a politics of ultimate fulfillment or what one enthusiast calls "a politics of eternity."[29] For such people civility is far too cool a notion. But will not "a politics of eternity" turn out to be another monolith? And don't we really need a civil politics for the present?

Are civil politics possible today? Can a civil society be established or maintained? That depends on at least two things: whether civil righteousness is possible and whether human fulfillment can be achieved through means other than the nation-state or some other political instrumentality.

"Meere" Moral Education

The early advocates of civil righteousness looked to "meere" moral education as a necessary means to attain that quality. The importance of this means has often been acknowledged in this country, but the subject itself has hardly been a top priority, either among educators or the public at large. Furthermore, when moral education has

28. D. W. Brogan, *Citizenship Today* (Chapel Hill: University of North Carolina Press, 1960), 4.

29. Theodore Roszak, *Where the Wasteland Ends: Politics and Transcendence in Postindustrial Society* (Garden City, N.Y.: Doubleday, 1972).

been advocated, it has too often been understood in terms of the indoctrination or inculcation of a particular system of morals, rather than the development of the human capacity for moral growth and the achievement of moral maturity in decision making.

There is a time-honored tradition in the West that assumes that every child is a moral philosopher and hence can become a morally mature decision maker. That tradition has its roots in the Socratic assumptions and method. Socrates assumed that knowledge is virtue, that to know the good leads one to do it. Knowledge, however, was not acquired so much by societal indoctrination—by a kind of pouring-in process—as it was by eliciting from the child what was already resident within him or her, by developing his or her innate human capacities. That tradition continues to live in some moral philosophy and education in our time, as we shall see in a particular instance, after a brief discussion of how it has been challenged and modified in Western history.

Skeptics have denied that there is finally any rationally demonstrable, morally right or wrong way in human decision making. Some, in the countertradition of Socrates' chief opponents, the Sophists, have specialized in shaping morality and moral argument to their own ends. They have sought to demonstrate that, given the final relativity and subjectivity of all moral decisions, any clever person can wrap his own selfish designs in a publicly acceptable cloak of moral rectitude. In this countertradition, moral education consists primarily in teaching the subservient to behave as those in control want them to behave.

While generally scorning this kind of relativism and cynicism, one type of Christian moral philosophy has pointed to another difficulty in achieving moral behavior. Rooted in the views of Saint Paul and subsequently developed by Saint Augustine and others, including the more orthodox Puritans, this tradition has stressed the role of the will in decision making. According to this view, to know the good is not necessarily to do it. As Paul put it: "I do not do what I want, but I do the very thing I hate."[30] What is required finally in overcoming the deep-seated effects of original sin is a change so profound as radically to reorient the inner man. Logically, in this view, there could be no moral development apart from this radical change. And politically this same logic might lead to the conclusion that only the saints—*i.e.*, those who had experienced the radical change—should rule. Some Christians, including some Puritans, followed this logic. But others, like Roger Williams, were more realistic in recognizing, on the one hand, that apparently people could develop morally and govern themselves in a provisionally peaceful way without having experienced saving grace and, on the other hand, that even the saints were less than morally perfect.

In effect, these people proposed or implied in their views two levels of righteousness. A *civil righteousness*, which could be achieved without the necessary realization of an ultimate saving righteousness, was minimally essential for human community and for a civil society in which a certain level of justice in human relations would be realized. Generally the realism of these Christians led them also to recognize that even the achievement of a proximate justice in this world required that human sinfulness be checked by law and that the lawmakers and administrators be checked by each other. A *saving righteousness*, something akin to Jonathan Edwards' "true virtue," could enable human beings to go the second mile and more in human relations. The end of saving righteousness was not justice, important as that was, but universal benevolence, the "beloved community" founded finally on selfless love. The task of "meere" moral education, in this view, was to focus on going the first mile—that is, enabling people to

30. Romans 7:15, Revised Standard Version.

practice "common honestie in matters of contract and traffique with men" or, to put it in an ancient prophetic form, to do justly in human relations.

What is suggested finally in this chapter is that this two-level view affords a cogent, realistic theoretical context for the achievement of civil politics. To develop this position further, I now turn to moral education in our time and to the Socratic tradition that still lives in some present-day moral theory. Specifically, the work and views of the Harvard moral psychologist Lawrence Kohlberg are cited in this connection.

Professor Kohlberg and his associates claim that their experimentation has demonstrated that there are universal human moral tendencies and stages of development, and they draw from this the conclusion that moral education should focus on the development of these tendencies through the various stages. The tendencies are *empathy*, which means concern for others, and *justice*, which means concern for equality and reciprocity in human relations. The stages are:

Level 1: *Premoral*
Stage 1: Punishment and obedience orientation
Stage 2: Naïve instrumental hedonism

Level 2: *Morality of Conventional Role Conformity*
Stage 3: Good-boy morality of maintaining good relations with others
Stage 4: Authority, rule- and order-maintaining morality

Level 3: *Morality of Self-Accepted Moral Principles*
Stage 5: Morality of contract, of individual rights, and of democratically accepted law
Stage 6: Morality of individual principles of conscience (moral autonomy)

These tendencies and stages, Kohlberg claims, are independent of cultural conditioning and of religion. In applying his findings to formal education, he argues that all children are moral philosophers and that all teachers should also be moral psychologists. Teachers should assist children in advancing through the various stages of moral development toward the ultimate goal of moral autonomy. Consequently, findings in this area of moral development merit a place alongside learning theory in teacher preparation and curriculum planning.[31]

This understanding of moral development is clearly compatible with the notion of civility, and the approach itself, if implemented in moral education, can be conducive to the achievement of civil politics. The approach is developmental, not indoctrinational. It seeks to help youngsters become consistent moral philosophers and achieve moral maturity. And, if consistently and thoroughly implemented, it should help to produce adults who are capable of self-government.

Attractive as it is, however, this view is not finally persuasive. Instead, I find the view of the Christian moralists alluded to above to be both more realistic and more fully human. To begin at an elementary level with Kohlberg's universal human tendencies: There may be universal tendencies to empathy and justice; clearly there are also

31. On the views and research of Lawrence Kohlberg see the following by Kohlberg: "Moral Development," *International Encyclopedia of the Social Sciences,* X, 483–94; "The Child as Moral Philosopher," *Psychology Today,* II (September, 1968), 25–30; "Stages of Moral Development as a Basis for Moral Education," in Clive M. Beck (ed.), *Moral Education: Interdisciplinary Approaches* (Toronto: University of Toronto Press, 1971), 23–92; "Moral Education in the Schools: A Developmental View," *School Review,* LXXIV (Spring, 1966), 1–30; "Development of Moral Character and Moral Ideology," in Martin L. Hoffman and Lois Wladis Hoffman (eds.), *Review of Child Development Research* (New York: Russell Sage Foundation, 1964), I, 383–431; with Elliot Turiel, "Moral Development and Moral Education," in Gerald S. Lesser (ed.), *Psychology and Educational Practice* (Glenview, Ill.: Scott, Foresman, 1971), 410–65; with Rochelle Mayer, "Development as the Aim of Education," *Harvard Educational Review,* XLIV (1972), 449–96; and with Carol Gilligan, "The Adolescent as a Philosopher: The Discovery of Self in a Postconventional World," *Daedalus* (Fall, 1971), 1051–86.

tendencies to self-interest and self-serving. The object of moral education should be to develop the former and to curb or redirect the latter. Civil society depends on the success of both efforts and probably also on a certain amount of seasoning with that realism that the Founding Fathers built into their civil polity. Reinhold Niebuhr's pithy summary is still very persuasive: "Man's capacity for justice makes democracy possible; but man's inclination to injustice makes democracy necessary."[32]

To turn to the other end of Kohlberg's theory, *i.e.*, the sixth stage and the ideal of the morally autonomous individual who is completely guided by internalized rational principles: This is a noble ideal. Clearly a community of morally autonomous individuals—in which all, not merely some, were philosopher-kings—is much to be desired. But to me the ideal is finally too individualistic, too cerebral, and too austere in what it implies about human potential and human fulfillment. It sees neither the need nor the desirability of transport and transformation, of the rebirth of soul that enables the self to find fulfillment beyond itself in a companionship that clearly transcends the bounds of civil society and that is outside the compass of "meere" moral education.

Seeking Soul

Not unlike the Founding Fathers, Professor Kohlberg regards religion institutionally as culture-bound and individually as "a private belief system." Curiously, he honors Martin Luther King, Jr., as a prime exemplar of Stage 6 morality, but Dr. King's religious experience and commitment are silently passed over.[33] But surely Dr. King was

32. Reinhold Niebuhr, *The Children of Light and the Children of Darkness: A Vindication of Democracy and a Critique of Its Traditional Defense* (New York: Charles Scribner's Sons, 1960), xiii.

33. See Kohlberg, "The Child as Moral Philosopher." See also Lawrence Kohlberg, "Moral and Religious Education and the Public Schools: A Developmental View," in Theodore R. Sizer (ed.), *Reli-*

moved by a powerful sense of divine imperative, an experience of communal love, and a religious faith that enabled him to live confidently and joyfully through great danger—even into death. He profoundly articulated and exemplified both civil and saving righteousness, and in so doing he testified to the reality of a power even greater than completely internalized, rational moral principles.

The civil state has no *direct* means available to it for producing men like Martin Luther King, Jr. It functions at its best through the indirect encouragement of such means—that is, by protecting the liberty to seek (and find) soul fulfillment. It should not impede that search either by claiming too much for itself or by proscribing spiritual experimentation short of the forceful disruption of civil order. The Founding Fathers were generally convinced that such liberty to seek would finally enhance the chances of civil society itself.[34]

---

gion and Public Education (Boston: Houghton Mifflin Company, 1967), 164–83. Recently Kohlberg has speculated about a possible seventh stage that may be unique to the elderly and involves adoption of a religious or cosmic perspective. See his "Stages and Aging in Moral Development—Some Speculations," *Gerontologist*, XIII (Winter, 1973), 497–502.

34. Benjamin Franklin supported a variety of religious groups because he thought they contributed to the public good. See his letter to Ezra Stiles, March 9, 1790: "All Sects here, and we have a great Variety, have experienced my good will in assisting them with Subscriptions for building their new Places of Worship." L. Jesse Lemisch (ed.), *Benjamin Franklin: The Autobiography and Other Writings* (New York: New American Library, 1961), 338. See also articles six through eight of James Madison's "Memorial and Remonstrance," as presented to the General Assembly of Virginia in 1785, in Norman Cousins (ed.), *In God We Trust: The Religious Beliefs and Ideas of the American Founding Fathers* (New York: Harper and Brothers, 1958), 311.

Conclusion: An Open End

Shortly before his death, after the long period of the conquest of Canaan and various attempts to deal with factionalism among the people of Israel, Joshua gathered the scattered tribes of Israel together at Shechem for a final, stirring reminder of their common heritage and a rousing call to a communal affirmation of their loyalty to their God. He capped his zealous appeal with an ultimate challenge to decide for the God of Israel over the gods of other peoples, and he dramatically pressed this challenge by proclaiming his own decision: "Choose this day whom you will serve . . . but as for me and my house, we will serve the Lord!"[1]

Such decisiveness and apparent clarity are appealing, especially at a time of communal crisis. There are those today who think that our choice as Americans is that clear and simple: Do what the Bible says and serve the Lord! But we live in a different time and place than Joshua did. First, it is not at all clear that one can even speak now for his whole house. Pluralism, secularism, and individualism

---

1. Joshua 24, especially verses 14–15, Revised Standard Version.

have invaded the household. We have, no doubt, over-stressed individualism in this country. We recognize today, as suggested in chapter two, the necessity and value of community, and we are aware that disintegration of such primary communities as the family seriously threatens our capacity to develop personal integrity. Hence some viable analogue for the whole house is needed. But we are not likely soon to return to an extended familial or a tribal culture. Nor should we lightly dismiss the values of a personal integrity, which, while rooted in communal soil, can rise above that soil. Unless we can somehow combine community with personal choice, we may be thrown into a situation worse than that primitive tribalism that pits group against group and which can stifle the individual human soul.

Second, what it means to serve the Lord is not as clear in our time as it seemingly was in Joshua's. That may be difficult enough for some of us to fathom as individuals. Politically, in the context of the nation, it is even more difficult to determine. I suggest as a sufficient working guideline the goal that has been central to the American vision of a genuinely civil society—an attempt to follow the powerful, prophetic admonition to "let justice roll down like waters."[2] But can we strive for justice without assuming, as Joshua did, that we are a chosen people destined to usher in the kingdom of God? Can people in fact seek to do justly without the added incentive that comes from knowing that they are on the Lord's side or, better still for them, that the Lord is on their side? Is it motive power enough to assume that *justice* is what the Lord desires in a civil community, even though it is not entirely clear what justice is at any particular instance and may even be less clear whether our particular course is the Lord's special, chosen way?

2. Amos 5:24, Revised Standard Version.

Joshua knew the way of the Lord; hence it was only a matter of practical politics for him to be able to lead his household and the people of Israel in that way. Countless political leaders who have come after him have had the same certainty. As we have seen, our Puritan forebears, with the exception of a few men like Roger Williams, shared that kind of conviction and believed that they as saints must rule if there was to be a godly or even peaceful commonwealth. What our American Founding Fathers did was to launch an unprecedented experiment, a society in which men of sharply different views on ultimate questions could live side by side. But that could happen only under the conditions that one group could not by force exterminate or completely dominate others and that the government itself would not be formally allied with any religious group. Religion, as commonly understood, was left basically on its own to sustain itself voluntarily, without governmental support, and to influence government more by indirect than direct means. Under these conditions the way was open for full and free religious search and expression. Some of the more forward-looking first citizens of the new nation confidently expected that both religion and civil society would benefit in this experiment.

With the launching of the experiment, the way was opened for a twofold development—a substantial increase in religious activity and a rising sense of excitement and confidence in the promise and uniqueness of the *novus ordo seclorum*. Formal disentanglement of religion from the state created a spiritual vacuum into which there could, and did, rush all kinds of religious claims, ventures, and experiments.[3] These challenged, activated, and in some cases no doubt satisfied the human search for soul. At the same time, the new nation itself, the very experi-

3. See, for example, Alice Felt Tyler, *Freedom's Ferment* (Minneapolis: University of Minnesota Press, 1944).

ment in launching a new society for this world, appealed
strongly to men's minds and hearts. It was an exciting and
hopeful venture of which to be a part. And this excitement
was a significant ingredient in the religious ferment of the
national period—*i.e.*, between the American Revolution
and the Civil War. In addition, however, confidence in the
uniqueness of the new venture took on a kind of religious
life of its own. It seemed possible that the *novus ordo
seclorum* might itself satisfy the human search for soul.

One of the questions that has confronted Americans
since is whether they could find a soul identity without
selling their souls to the nation as redeemer. Or, to put it
another way: Could the excitement of the venture be
maintained and its promise realized without making ultimate claims for that venture itself? Or did the very success
of the American experiment require that it be proclaimed
and embraced as unique, divinely destined, and the last,
best human hope? And, if that were the case, was the
experiment in launching a *civil* society really a success?

Some scholars have argued that, in fact, there did develop in America a political or civil religion, which assumed an institutional life of its own alongside that of
churches, sects, and denominations that are more commonly recognized as religious institutions. And debate has
gone on among scholars about the status of this "civil
religion."[4] I have expressed some doubts, in chapter four,
about the extent of the formalization of such a religion in
the early days of the Republic. Furthermore, it seems
evident that if such a religion did or does exist it would be

4. On the "civil religion" debate see Robert N. Bellah, "Civil
Religion in America," with commentaries by others and a response
by Bellah, in Donald R. Cutler (ed.), *The Religious Situation, 1968*
(Boston: Beacon Press, 1968), 331–93. Professor Bellah's seminal
essay has also been published in various other places, and the notion
of "civil religion" has entered the vocabulary of scholars of religion
in America. For a critical view, however, see John F. Wilson, "The
Status of Civil Religion in America," in Elwyn A. Smith (ed.), *The*

consonant with the American civil polity only if it made no final claims for itself and for the nation of which it is an expression. Indeed, at its best, a *civil* religion should remind the nation of its essentially civil creed and reinforce the quest for civil righteousness. And, finally, it should not preclude full and free religious expression. But one wonders how possible this kind of moderation is in a time of frustration and ferment, when state power is greater than it has ever been and when the people may be urged with increasing forcefulness to rally around the banner of national uniqueness and destiny.

What has been most significant and distinctive about the American quest for soul, however, is not the emergence of a civil religion but rather a peculiar mixture of (1) religious and secular expectation and hope, (2) a predominant religious stress on experiential spirituality, (3) formal constitutional support of free religious search and expression, and (4) a civil view of the limited spiritual role of the nation-state. This combination has given rise to unprecedented religious fermentation and experimentation and to considerable spiritual vitality in this country. Vitality is threatened, however, as any element disappears from the mix or is seriously truncated—as expectation declines and hope gives way to despair or cynicism, as spirituality is weakened, as the integrity of civil society is threatened, and as the nation itself assumes or is assigned an increasingly more important spiritual role. Today all of these things are evident in varying degrees. But there are also hopeful signs among us, signs that the experiment is going on and may continue to go on with vigor.

There is reason to hope, for example, that the whole

Religion of the Republic (Philadelphia: Fortress Press, 1971), 1–21. Sociologist Robin M. Williams, Jr., states that "every functioning society has to an important degree a common religion," in his *American Society: A Sociological Interpretation* (2nd ed.; New York: Knopf, 1960), 332.

series of developments lumped together under the heading "Watergate" may have a positive long-range effect. Possibly this experience might result, among other things, in a renewed commitment to the means and ends of the American civil experiment. Perhaps the needed rallying public figure for our time, then, is not primarily a Joshua—*i.e.*, a man of conviction and charisma who can rally his people to the banner of the Lord. Perhaps it is rather an assembly of representative figures, fallible human beings, who can reissue a call on behalf of "we the people of the United States" to renew our commitment to seek to "establish Justice, insure domestic Tranquillity, provide for the common defence, promote the general Welfare, and secure the Blessings of Liberty to ourselves and our Posterity."[5]

One may also find reason for hope in the very ferment that characterizes the current religious scene in America. Our age resembles the national period in its outpouring of religious pursuits. Today, in fact, when almost every religious system known to man is being tried in this country, the range of religious experimentation is considerably greater than it was in that earlier period. The American civil experiment in the constitutional encouragement of religious search and expression has obviously been a success in this regard at least.

This is not to suggest that ferment in and of itself effects positive results, either individually or for the larger community. Some avenues of spiritual quest may lead only to spiritual dead ends, while others may lead to greater maturity. To determine whether one form of spiritual search will have a more positive effect than another is no simple matter, because of the subjectivity involved and because the outcome may be beyond our present ken. Nevertheless, we may and indeed must hazard certain judgments.

Resemblance to the early decades of the new nation

5. *United States Constitution*, Preamble.

ceases when one looks at the causes, the context, and the possible effects of present seeking. Today, for example, the national mood is much less exuberant, expectant, and optimistic, and the current quest seems to be more desperate than was that of a seemingly happier time. Some have despaired of this present world, and they want out. This is evident in a self-centered quest that ignores social issues. It is also evident in a dark, apocalyptic outlook, which, in contrast to the optimistic eschatology of the earlier period, forecasts nothing but doom for this world. At the same time the present search also appears to be more sweeping and more primal than was that which went on in a time of national innocence. One can hope that this quest might also be more profound in its effects. Perhaps some seekers will tap the wellsprings of spiritual renewal and a new birth of dynamic religion may result. We may in the long run secure a grasp on reality that is better able to cope creatively with public issues than was the age that gave way to the American Civil War.

Such a possibility becomes less likely, however, as people are willing and even eager to foreclose or foreshorten spiritual quest, as they avidly settle on quick answers to human aspirations and shortcuts to human fulfillment. The very vitality of the American search for soul has depended to no small extent on the quality of openness in the American environment and outlook. Theologically, God has been understood as a transcendent deity who is beyond human confinement and who, as the Pilgrim pastor John Robinson put it, has still more truth to disclose. [6] God has also been understood as an immanent deity who, or whose grace, can be experienced as a dynamic, transforming reality in this life. Temporally, the future has generally been seen as pregnant with the promise of better

6. See Cotton Mather, *Magnalia Christi Americana*, ed. Thomas Robbins *et al.* (New York: Russell and Russell, 1967), I, 64.

things, as a time of rebirth in contrast to the moribund past. And the present may be seen as affording a foretaste of that promised fulfillment. Spatially, the new continent has invited men to leave the restrictions of confined space and to try new ventures. Formally and constitutionally, the Republic has, from its beginnings, supported religious liberty and hence given relatively free reign to varieties of religious and spiritual experience and experiment. Even communally, America has tended to be conducive to openness, in part because of the sheer necessities of a pluralistic reality and in part out of conscious universalistic affirmations.

At the same time, however, spiritual vitality has often been undercut or discouraged in America by closed ideologies, narrow loyalties, limited horizons, excessive concern with "making it," and temptation to succumb to the "quick sell." The circle of human consciousness has too easily been a tight and constrictive enclosure. Other people have been shut out or used. Other living things have been degraded. The physical environment has been ruthlessly exploited. And the very notion of the *novus ordo seclorum* has, in fact, sometimes given rise to a sense of superiority and chosenness, which, while supportive of self-confidence and soul certainty, has also narrowed the circle of consciousness.

The problem we face in our search for soul is to find a proper balance between openness and the integrity of identity and commitment. People need not only to be seekers; they need also to be finders. But, to use those words of child's play—which admittedly are not always merely words or sentiments confined to children or to play—need finders be keepers? To be spiritually satisfied, must we know that we have found *the* way—the one way, the only way, and the whole way?

In the trials that may well await us all, spiritual certainty could outlast spiritual openness. Nevertheless, for some of us at least, the search must go on. That does not necessarily mean that one blows in the wind like a weather vane. Indeed, the final test of spiritual maturity is, in the words of Erik Erikson, sober and even glad acceptance of one's "one and only life cycle as something that had to be and that, by necessity, permitted of no substitution" within the context of an awareness of "the relativity of all the various life styles which have given meaning to human striving" and a "comradeship with the ordering ways of distant times and different pursuits."[7]

7. Erik Erikson, *Childhood and Society* (Middlesex, England: Penguin Books, 1965), 260, in connection with his description of the "ego integrity," which may be characteristic of a realized human maturity. Erikson sees that integrity, which he associates with the eighth and final stage of human development, as being in tension with "despair."

Bibliographical Essay

Americans have been looking at themselves since the first English settlers became Americans. Indeed, these Englishmen were much in the habit of self-examination before they landed on the eastern shores of North America. There is an extensive literature on this subject of the self and self-examination in America. The following works are some that I have found especially suggestive.

Owen C. Watkins, *The Puritan Experience: Studies in Spiritual Autobiography* (New York: Schocken Books, 1972), and Margaret Bottrall, *Every Man a Phoenix: Studies in Seventeenth Century Autobiography* (London: Murray, 1958), deal with English Puritans of the seventeenth century who are so important as stage setters for self-perception among the early Americans. Norman Pettit and Daniel B. Shea, Jr., examine the American Puritans in *The Heart Prepared: Grace and Conversion in Puritan Spiritual Life* (New Haven: Yale University Press, 1966) and *Spiritual Autobiography in Early America* (Princeton: Princeton University Press, 1968), respectively. John N. Morris analyzes the role of crisis and radical inner change in the emergence of self among selected English figures from John Bunyan and George Fox to the romantics in *Versions of the Self: Studies in English Autobiography from John Bunyan to John Stuart Mill* (New York: Basic Books, 1966). The emergence of the individual who experiences little need to see himself in community is examined by Robert F. Sayre in *The Examined Self: Benjamin Franklin, Henry Adams, Henry James* (Princeton: Princeton University Press, 1964). E. Fred Carlisle treats an individual for whom such a process was both exhilarating and problematic in *The Uncertain Self: Whitman's Drama of Identity* (East Lansing: Michigan State University Press, 1973). And Wylie Sypher signals the end of such individuality in his *Loss of the Self in Modern Literature and Art* (New York: Random House, 1962). The above works are based primarily on literary sources. T. R. Young attempts a sociological analysis of recent trends in his *New Sources of Self* (New York: Pergamon Press, 1972).

American self-examination and self-perception have been continually aided and abetted by a host of foreign visitors and articulate foreigners who came to stay, from Michel de Crèvecœur, the French settler whose *Letters from an American Farmer* were first published in the late eighteenth century, to Alistair Cooke, the sympathetic and perceptive British-born observer who, through the media of television and the printed word—*America* (New York: Knopf, 1973)—has recently shared publicly his perspective on this country. Among the more well-known works by foreign observers are Alexis de Tocqueville's *Democracy in America*, first published in 1835; Lord James Bryce's *The American Commonwealth*, first published in 1891; and D. W. Brogan's *The American Character*, published in 1944 and 1956. All of these contain valuable insights on the religious as well as other aspects of American self-perception. Others, who out of their own backgrounds, interests, and qualifications produced perceptive analyses of spiritual and religious aspects of the American character and self-understanding, include Philip Schaff, *America: A Sketch of Its Political, Social, and Religious Character,* ed. Perry Miller (Cambridge: Harvard University Press, 1961); George Santayana, *Character and Opinion in the United States: With Reminiscences of William James and Josiah Royce and Academic Life in America* (New York: Charles Scribner's Sons, 1920); André Siegfried, *America Comes of Age: A French Analysis* (New York: Harcourt, Brace and Company, 1927); and Jacques Maritain, *Reflections on America* (New York: Charles Scribner's Sons, 1958). Under the title *The Voluntary Church: American Religious Life (1740–1865) Seen Through the Eyes of European Visitors* (New York: Macmillan Company, 1967), Milton B. Powell has assembled selected comments relative to American religious life made by eighteen foreign visitors or immigrants during this formative period. His collection includes selections from Crèvecoeur, Tocqueville, and Schaff. The Belgian Count Eugène Goblet d'Alviella, professor of comparative theology at the University of Brussels, studied "religious progress" in this country in the early 1880s and published his observations in *The Contemporary Evolution of Religious Thought in England, America, and India,* trans. J. Moden (London: Williams and Norgate, 1885). The work deals with liberalizing movements such as transcendentalism, Unitarianism, "free religion," and "the religion of evolution."

The notion of the American as a new man was stated relatively early by Crèvecoeur in his letter "What is an American?" in *Letters from an American Farmer* (New York: E. P. Dutton and Company, 1951). Newness was often understood to mean a return to innocence, an entry into paradise, or the realization of the kingdom of God. On these themes see Mircea Eliade, "Paradise and Utopia," in his *The Quest: History and Meaning in Religion* (Chicago: University of Chicago Press, 1969); R. W. B. Lewis, *The American Adam: Innocence, Tragedy, and Tradition*

in the Nineteenth Century (Chicago: University of Chicago
Press, 1955); Norman Cohn, *The Pursuit of the Millen-
nium: Revolutionary Millenarians and Mystical Anarchists
of the Middle Ages* (London: Secker and Warburg, Ltd.,
1957; Paladin, 1970); George H. Williams, *Wilderness and
Paradise in Christian Thought* (New York: Harper, 1962);
H. Richard Niebuhr, *The Kingdom of God in America*
(Chicago: Willett, Clark and Company, 1937); and Charles
L. Sanford, *The Quest for Paradise: Europe and the Ameri-
can Moral Imagination* (Urbana: University of Illinois
Press, 1961).

Confidence and optimism have been common qualities
in America, as has a sense of peculiar destiny. Tom Paine
was perhaps the first to articulate these notions widely for
the common man. In his *Common Sense* he compared the
American opportunity for new beginning with that of
the period following Noah and the great flood. For a systematic treatment of some of the religious roots and aspects
of American self-confidence, see Ernest Lee Tuveson, *Redeemer Nation: The Idea of America's Millennial Role*
(Chicago: University of Chicago Press, 1968). And for a
thoughtful and thorough treatment of the relationship
between religious and political identity in America see
Cushing Strout, *The New Heavens and New Earth: Political Religion in America* (New York: Harper and Row,
1974).

The United States has been described as a nation of
immigrants. Clearly migration, the movement from one
place to another and from one cultural context to another,
has both characterized and affected the American search
for soul. On immigration I am heavily dependent on Oscar
Handlin's classical treatment, *The Uprooted* (lst ed.; Grosset and Dunlap, 1951), supplemented by some familiarity
with original sources such as autobiographies and novels. I
have also used the works of such well-known scholars of
immigration as Theodore C. Blegen, Marcus Lee Hansen,

and Carl F. Wittke and the following: Oscar Handlin (ed.), *Children of the Uprooted* (New York: G. Brazziller, 1966) and *Immigration as a Factor in American History* (Englewood Cliffs, N.J.: Prentice-Hall, 1959); Henry Steele Commager (ed.), *Immigration and American History: Essays in Honor of Theodore C. Blegen* (Minneapolis: University of Minnesota Press, 1961); Robert E. Park and Herbert A. Miller, *Old World Traits Transplanted* (New York: Harper and Brothers, 1921); and Edmund Traverso, *Immigration: A Study in American Values* (Boston: Heath, 1964). On the subject of Americanization I have found John Higham, *Strangers in the Land: Patterns of American Nativism* (New York: Atheneum, 1963), especially useful. See also Edward George Hartman, *The Movement to Americanize the Immigrant* (New York: A. M. S. Press, 1967), and my own essay, "Americanization: Sacred or Profane Phenomenon?" *Reconstructionist*, May 7, 1971, reprinted in Martin E. Marty and Dean G. Peerman (eds.), *New Theology No. 9* (New York: Macmillan Company, 1972).

On the impact on American self-perception of space, the frontier, and the ever-present pressure toward mobility, I find the following especially perceptive: Sidney E. Mead, "The American People: Their Space, Time, and Religion," *The Lively Experiment: The Shaping of Christianity in America* (New York: Harper and Row, 1963), Chap. 1; and Erik H. Erikson, "Reflections on the American Identity," *Childhood and Society* (Middlesex, England: Penguin Books, 1965), Chap. 8 and "Identity and Uprootedness in Our Time," *Insight and Responsibility: Lectures on the Ethical Implications of Psychoanalytic Insight* (New York: W. W. Norton, 1964), Chap. 3.

On the quest for unity or peoplehood in America see Paul C. Nagel, *One Nation Indivisible: The Union in American Thought, 1776–1861* (New York: Oxford University Press, 1964) and *This Sacred Trust: American Nationality, 1798–1898* (New York: Oxford University Press, 1971).

The restlessness that inspires human mobility and search may be understood to be at root spiritual in nature. Our souls are restless until they find rest in God, declared Saint Augustine. The major tradition of American spirituality has stressed both the necessity and the human difficulty of achieving the ultimate transformation that signals arrival at that destination. Nevertheless, although it requires a miracle, that transformation has seemed possible in the form of an experience beyond comparison. American Puritan approaches to that experience are discussed by Norman Pettit in *The Heart Prepared: Grace and Conversion in Puritan Spiritual Life* (New Haven: Yale University Press, 1966). For some indication of the effects of this sort of view on self-perception see the works of Bottrall, Morris, Shea, and Watkins cited previously.

Perhaps the most skilled analyst of the experience of saving faith or grace that America has produced, and certainly one of the most systematic surveyors of that phenomenon, was Jonathan Edwards. See in particular his *A Treatise Concerning the Religious Affections*, which has been critically edited by John E. Smith (New Haven: Yale University Press, 1959). The other directly relevant treatises by Edwards on religious experience are: "A Faithful Narrative of the Surprising Work of God in the Conversion of Many Hundred Souls," "The Distinguishing Marks of a Work of the Spirit of God," and "Some Thoughts Concerning the Present Revival of Religion in New England." All three of these are available in the volume edited by C. C. Goen under the title *The Works of Jonathan Edwards: The Great Awakening* (New Haven: Yale University Press, 1972). Selections from these and other works by Edwards are available in Clarence H. Faust and Thomas H. Johnson (eds.), *Jonathan Edwards: Representative Selections* (New York: American Book Company, 1962), and in Ola Elizabeth Winslow (ed.), *Jonathan Edwards: Basic Writings* (New York: New American Library, 1966).

R. A. Knox has dealt historically and systematically with the "religion of experience" in his classical work *Enthusiasm: A Chapter in the History of Religion, with Special Reference to the XVII and XVIII Centuries* (Oxford: Oxford University Press, 1962). Edwards smarted under the charge of "enthusiasm"; it was not a good word. Nevertheless, he finally accepted it if the kind of experience he had witnessed and perhaps even had had himself was meant by that word. On this point see David S. Lovejoy (ed.), *Religious Enthusiasm and the Great Awakening* (Englewood Cliffs, N.J.: Prentice-Hall, 1969). And for Edwards, as for his Puritan predecessors and his evangelical successors, while man might not become so God filled as to cease to be man, he could only become fully human through a divinely empowered and directly experienced act of saving faith.

The classic American treatment of the regeneration experience, after Edwards' works, is William James's *The Varieties of Religious Experience*, first published in 1902 with many subsequent printings. James distinguished between "once-born" and "twice-born" types. The latter is characteristic of what I have called the major tradition of American spirituality. The "once-born" type is characteristic of another tradition of American spirituality that, being persuaded of continuity between God and man, has stressed the relative ease of ultimate transformation or fulfillment. That tradition is perhaps most articulately represented by Emerson and other transcendentalists. For Emerson, see, for example, his "Divinity School Address" of 1838 and his essay "Nature" of 1836. On the transcendentalists see Perry Miller (ed.), *The Transcendentalists: An Anthology* (Cambridge: Harvard University Press, 1950). See also Miller's perceptive essay "From Edwards to Emerson" in the *New England Quarterly*, XIII (1940), 589–617, reprinted in his book *Errand into the Wilderness* (Cambridge: Harvard University Press, 1956), and an earlier suggestive essay on the same theme—William W. Fenn, "The Unitarians," in *The Religious History of New England* (Cambridge: Harvard University Press, 1917), 97–133.

Each of the two traditions of spirituality mentioned above could be, and was, devalued—the one into a religion of morality and rules, which, if it stressed transformation at all, conceived of it as being analogous to a business deal, and the other into a pollyanna view of life troubled by neither longing nor death. H. Richard Niebuhr had this sort of devaluation in mind when he wrote of "evolutionary optimism" that a "God without wrath brought men without sin into a kingdom without judgment through the ministrations of a Christ without a cross," in connection with his analysis, "Institutionalization and Secularization," in *The Kingdom of God in America*. See also Donald Meyer, *The Positive Thinkers: A Study of the American Quest for Health, Wealth, and Personal Power from Mary Baker Eddy to Norman Vincent Peale* (Garden City, N.Y.: Doubleday, 1965).

Some early Americans believed that there was an inseparable link between the sought-after spiritual transformation and a functioning civil society. Hence, in some of the early Puritan commonwealths, only men who could convincingly demonstrate that they had had the saving experience were allowed to vote and to govern. Other people were abided in the commonwealth only if they behaved themselves morally and refrained from advocating false doctrines. For both religious and political reasons Roger Williams advocated soul liberty against this view. Full understanding of the nature and significance of Williams' views does not come easily, and entry into the thicket of interpretation of Williams requires courage or foolhardiness. Perhaps no other American has been so much subjected to revisionism. Scholars during the early twentieth century generally regarded him as an "irrepressible democrat" whose primary concerns were political in nature. In this connection see, for example, Samuel H. Brockunier, *The Irrepressible Democrat: Roger Williams* (New York: Ronald Press Company, 1920); James Ernst, *The Political Thought of Roger Williams* (Seattle: University of Washington Press, 1929); and Vernon L. Parrington, *Main Currents in American Thought: An Interpretation of American Literature from the Beginning to 1920* (New York: Harcourt, Brace and Company, 1927).

More recently scholars have rediscovered that Williams was, after all, a religious man. Perhaps the most decisive and influential work of this sort was that done by Mauro Calamandrei and reported succinctly in "Neglected Aspects of Roger Williams' Thought," *Church History*, XXI (1952), 239–58. Also of considerable importance in this recent revision in Williams scholarship are the works of Perry Miller, two of which are cited below, and Alan Simpson, "How Democratic was Roger Williams?" *William and Mary Quarterly*, XIII (1956), 53–67. But Williams was no ordinary religious man, nor were his religious convictions conventional in his time or typical of his age. These convictions and the searchings to which they gave rise led Williams to endeavor to establish a civil state that permitted maximum freedom of conscience within the limits of civil order and complete dissociation of church and state. In that he was unique in his time. For a succinct survey of the treatment of Williams by the scholars, see LeRoy Moore, Jr., "Roger Williams and the Historians," *Church History*, XXXII (1963), 432–51. With the republication of the Narragansett edition of the *Complete Writings of Roger Williams* in six volumes, with the addition of a seventh volume containing new materials and an introduction by Perry Miller (New York: Russell and Russell, 1963), the writings of this significant and enigmatic seventeenth-century figure became more readily available.

Williams' style and thought are still not easily handled,

however. Works that I have found helpful, in addition to
the articles by Calamandrei and Simpson cited above,
include Perry Miller's introduction to the *Complete Writ-
ings of Roger Williams*, VII, 5–25, and his *Roger Williams:
His Contributions to the American Tradition* (New York:
Atheneum, 1965); John Garrett, *Roger Williams: Witness
Beyond Christendom, 1603–1683* (New York: Macmillan
Company, 1970); Edmund S. Morgan, *Roger Williams, the
Church, and the State* (New York: Harcourt, Brace and
World, 1967); and Ola Elizabeth Winslow, *Master Roger
Williams: A Biography* (New York: Macmillan Company,
1957).

Index